Edexcel

Poetry Anthology

For Advanced Subsidiary and Advanced GCE
examinations in English Literature and
English Language and Literature

Preface

The Edexcel Poetry Anthology has been produced to provide optional texts for teachers of the Edexcel Advanced Subsidiary and Advanced GCE English Literature and English Language and Literature specifications for 2001(AS) and 2002 (Advanced). The Anthology is in two sections: Section 1, Post-1770 Poetry, and Section 2, Pre-1770 Poetry.

Section 1 of the Anthology is an optional text for Unit 2, Drama and Poetry (Section B: Poetry), of the Advanced Subsidiary examination for English Literature. Section 2 of the Anthology is an optional text for Unit 5, Poetry and Drama (Section A: Pre-1770 Poetry), of the Advanced GCE examination for English Literature.

Section 1 of the Anthology is also an optional text for Unit 5, Wider Reading (Section B: Modern Literature), of the Advanced GCE examination for English Language and Literature. Section 2 of the Anthology is also an optional text for Unit 5, Wider Reading (Section A: Pre-1770 Poetry), of the Advanced GCE examination in English Language and Literature.

The Anthology thus provides two of the minimum of eight texts required for study for the Advanced GCE English Literature examination and two of the minimum of four texts required for study for the Advanced GCE English Language and Literature examination. The Anthology is however an optional text and may be used as a support for the teaching of poetry by teachers who do not wish to use it as a set text or texts for the specifications.

Both sections of the Anthology aim to provide a general introduction to the poetry of the periods concerned, and are organised on an approximately chronological basis. Section 1 contains an element of choice for teachers in the poems to be studied.

A separate Guide to the Edexcel Poetry Anthology has been produced to give background information on the poets and the poems in the Anthology. The Guide also provides suggested activities and questions for students.

Contents

Section One: Post-1770

Candidates must study *four* of the following groups of poems:

The Romantics

The Victorians

1900 – 1950

1950 – present

Poetry Around the World

Section Two: Pre-1770

Candidates must study *all five* of the following groups of poems:

Ballads

Tudor and Elizabethan Verse

Mostly Metaphysical Verse

17th Century

18th Century

Section One: Post-1770

The Romantics

London

I wander thro' each charter'd street,
Near where the charter'd Thames does flow,
And mark in every face I meet
Marks of weakness, marks of woe.

5 In every cry of every man,
In every Infant's cry of fear,
In every voice, in every ban,
The mind-forg'd manacles I hear.

How the Chimney-sweeper's cry
10 Every black'ning Church appalls;
And the hapless Soldier's sigh
Runs in blood down Palace walls.

But most thro' midnight streets I hear
How the youthful Harlot's curse
15 Blasts the new-born Infant's tear,
And blights with plagues the Marriage hearse.

William Blake

A Red, Red Rose

O my luve's like a red, red rose,
    That's newly sprung in June;
O my luve's like the melodie
    That's sweetly played in tune.

5 As fair art thou, my bonnie lass,
    So deep in luve am I;
And I will luve thee still, my dear,
    Till a' the seas gang dry.

Till a' the seas gang dry, my dear,
10   And the rocks melt wi' the sun:
O I will love thee still, my dear,
    While the sands o' life shall run.

And fare thee weel, my only luve,
    And fare thee weel awhile!
15 And I will come again, my luve,
    Though it were ten thousand mile.

Robert Burns

Composed upon Westminster Bridge, September 3, 1802

Earth has not anything to show more fair:
Dull would he be of soul who could pass by
A sight so touching in its majesty;
This City now doth, like a garment, wear
5 The beauty of the morning; silent, bare,
Ships, towers, domes, theatres, and temples lie
Open unto the fields, and to the sky;
All bright and glittering in the smokeless air.
Never did sun more beautifully steep
10 In his first splendour, valley, rock, or hill;
Ne'er saw I, never felt, a calm so deep!
The river glideth at his own sweet will:
Dear God! the very houses seem asleep;
And all that mighty heart is lying still!

William Wordsworth

Kubla Khan

In Xanadu did Kubla Khan
A stately pleasure dome decree:
Where Alph, the sacred river, ran
Through caverns measureless to man
5   Down to a sunless sea.
So twice five miles of fertile ground
With walls and towers were girdled round:
And there were gardens bright with sinuous rills,
Where blossomed many an incense-bearing tree;
10 And here were forests ancient as the hills,
Enfolding sunny spots of greenery.

But oh! that deep romantic chasm which slanted
Down the green hill athwart a cedarn cover!
A savage place! as holy and enchanted
15 As e'er beneath a waning moon was haunted
By woman wailing for her demon lover!
And from this chasm, with ceaseless turmoil seething
As if this earth in fast thick pants were breathing,
A mighty fountain momently was forced:
20 Amid whose swift half-intermitted burst
Huge fragments vaulted like rebounding hail,
Or chaffy grain beneath the thresher's flail:
And 'mid these dancing rocks at once and ever
It flung up momently the sacred river.
25 Five miles meandering with a mazy motion
Through wood and dale the sacred river ran,
Then reached the caverns measureless to man,
And sank in tumult to a lifeless ocean:
And 'mid this tumult Kubla heard from far
30 Ancestral voices prophesying war!

The shadow of the dome of pleasure
Floated midway on the waves;
Where was heard the mingled measure
From the fountain and the caves.
35 It was a miracle of rare device,
A sunny pleasure dome with caves of ice!

A damsel with a dulcimer
In a vision once I saw:
It was an Abyssinian maid,
40 And on her dulcimer she played,
Singing of Mount Abora.
Could I revive within me
Her symphony and song,
To such a deep delight 'twould win me,
45 That with music loud and long,
I would build that dome in air,
That sunny dome! those caves of ice!
And all who heard should see them there,
And all should cry, Beware! Beware!
50 His flashing eyes, his floating hair!
Weave a circle round him thrice,
And close your eyes with holy dread,
For he on honey-dew hath fed,
And drunk the milk of Paradise.

Samuel Taylor Coleridge

So We'll Go No More A-Roving

So we'll go no more a-roving
    So late into the night,
Though the heart be still as loving,
    And the moon be still as bright.

5 For the sword outwears its sheath,
    And the soul wears out the breast,
And the heart must pause to breathe,
    And Love itself have rest.

Though the night was made for loving,
10   And the day returns too soon,
Yet we'll go no more a-roving
    By the light of the moon.

Lord Byron

Lord Byron

To Autumn

Season of mists and mellow fruitfulness,
    Close bosom-friend of the maturing sun;
Conspiring with him how to load and bless
    With fruit the vines that round the thatch-eaves run;
5 To bend with apples the mossed cottage-trees,
    And fill all fruit with ripeness to the core;
        To swell the gourd, and plump the hazel shells
    With a sweet kernel; to set budding more,
And still more, later flowers for the bees,
10 Until they think warm days will never cease,
        For Summer has o'er-brimmed their clammy cells.

Who hath not seen thee oft amid thy store?
    Sometimes whoever seeks abroad may find
Thee sitting careless on a granary floor,
15   Thy hair soft-lifted by the winnowing wind;
Or on a half-reaped furrow sound asleep,
    Drowsed with the fume of poppies, while thy hook
        Spares the next swath and all its twinéd flowers:
And sometimes like a gleaner thou dost keep
20   Steady thy laden head across a brook;
    Or by a cider-press, with patient look,
        Thou watchest the last oozings hours by hours.

Where are the songs of Spring? Aye, where are they?
    Think not of them, thou hast thy music too –
25 While barréd clouds bloom the soft-dying day,
    And touch the stubble-plains with rosy hue;
Then in a wailful choir the small gnats mourn
    Among the river sallows, borne aloft
        Or sinking as the light wind lives or dies;
30 And full-grown lambs loud bleat from hilly bourn;
    Hedge crickets sing; and now with treble soft
    The redbreast whistles from a garden-croft;
        And gathering swallows twitter in the skies.

John Keats

I Am

I am: yet what I am none cares or knows,
    My friends forsake me like a memory lost,
I am the self-consumer of my woes –
    They rise and vanish in oblivious host,
5 Like shadows in love's frenzied, stifled throes –
And yet I am, and live – like vapours tossed

Into the nothingness of scorn and noise,
    Into the living sea of waking dreams,
Where there is neither sense of life or joys,
10   But the vast shipwreck of my life's esteems;
Even the dearest, that I love the best,
Are strange – nay, rather stranger than the rest.

I long for scenes, where man hath never trod,
    A place where woman never smiled or wept –
15 There to abide with my Creator, God,
    And sleep as I in childhood sweetly slept,
Untroubling, and untroubled where I lie,
The grass below – above the vaulted sky.

John Clare

To a Skylark

Hail to thee, blithe Spirit!
    Bird thou never wert,
That from Heaven, or near it,
    Pourest thy full heart
5 In profuse strains of unpremeditated art.

    Higher still and higher
    From the earth thou springest
Like a cloud of fire;
    The blue deep thou wingest,
10 And singing still dost soar, and soaring ever singest.

    In the golden lightning
    Of the sunken sun,
O'er which clouds are bright'ning,
    Thou dost float and run;
15 Like an unbodied joy whose race is just begun.

    The pale purple even
    Melts around thy flight;
Like a star of Heaven,
    In the broad daylight
20 Thou art unseen, but yet I hear thy shrill delight,

    Keen as are the arrows
    Of that silver sphere,
Whose intense lamp narrows
    In the white dawn clear
25 Until we hardly see – we feel that it is there.

    All the earth and air
    With thy voice is loud,
As, when night is bare,
    From one lonely cloud
30 The moon rains out her beams, and Heaven is overflowed.

    What thou art we know not;
    What is most like thee?
From rainbow clouds there flow not
    Drops so bright to see
35 As from thy presence showers a rain of melody.

    Like a Poet hidden
    In the light of thought,
Singing hymns unbidden,
    Till the world is wrought
40 To sympathy with hopes and fears it heeded not:

Like a high-born maiden
    In a palace tower,
Soothing her love-laden
    Soul in secret hour
45 With music sweet as love, which overflows her bower:

Like a glowworm golden
    In a dell of dew,
Scattering unbeholden
    Its aërial hue
50 Among the flowers and grass, which screen it from the view!

Like a rose embowered
    In its own green leaves,
By warm winds deflowered,
    Till the scent it gives
55 Makes faint with too much sweet those heavy-wingéd thieves:

Sound of vernal showers
    On the twinkling grass,
Rain-awakened flowers,
    All that ever was
60 Joyous, and clear, and fresh, thy music doth surpass:

Teach us, Sprite or Bird,
    What sweet thoughts are thine:
I have never heard
    Praise of love or wine
65 That panted forth a flood of rapture so divine.

Chorus Hymeneal,
    Or triumphal chant,
Matched with thine would be all
    But an empty vaunt,
70 A thing wherein we feel there is some hidden want.

What objects are the fountains
    Of thy happy strain?
What fields, or waves, or mountains?
    What shapes of sky or plain?
75 What love of thine own kind? what ignorance of pain?

With thy clear keen joyance
    Languor cannot be:
Shadow of annoyance
    Never came near thee:
80 Thou lovest – but ne'er knew love's sad satiety.

Waking or asleep,
    Thou of death must deem
Things more true and deep
    Than we mortals dream,
85 Or how could thy notes flow in such crystal stream?

We look before and after,
    And pine for what is not:
Our sincerest laughter
    With some pain is fraught;
90 Our sweetest songs are those that tell of saddest thought.

Yet if we could scorn
    Hate, and pride, and fear;
If we were things born
    Not to shed a tear,
95 I know not how thy joy we ever should come near.

Better than all measures
    Of delightful sound,
Better than all treasures
    That in books are found,
100 Thy skill to poet were, thou scorner of the ground!

Teach me half the gladness
    That thy brain must know,
Such harmonious madness
    From my lips would flow
105 The world should listen then – as I am listening now.

Percy Bysshe Shelley

The Victorians

Dover Beach

The sea is calm tonight.
The tide is full, the moon lies fair
Upon the straits; on the French coast the light
Gleams and is gone; the cliffs of England stand,
5 Glimmering and vast, out in the tranquil bay.
Come to the window, sweet is the night-air!
Only, from the long line of spray
Where the sea meets the moon-blanched land,
Listen! you hear the grating roar
10 Of pebbles which the waves draw back, and fling,
At their return, up the high strand,
Begin, and cease, and then again begin,
With tremulous cadence slow, and bring
The eternal note of sadness in.

15 Sophocles long ago
Heard it on the Aegean, and it brought
Into his mind the turbid ebb and flow
Of human misery; we
Find also in the sound a thought,
20 Hearing it by this distant northern sea.

The Sea of Faith
Was once, too, at the full, and round earth's shore
Lay like the folds of a bright girdle furled.
But now I only hear
25 Its melancholy, long, withdrawing roar,
Retreating, to the breath
Of the night-wind, down the vast edges drear
And naked shingles of the world.

Ah, love, let us be true
30 To one another! for the world, which seems
To lie before us like a land of dreams,
So various, so beautiful, so new,
Hath really neither joy, nor love, nor light,
Nor certitude, nor peace, nor help for pain;
35 And we are here as on a darkling plain
Swept with confused alarms of struggle and flight,
Where ignorant armies clash by night.

Matthew Arnold

Sonnets from the Portuguese XLIII

How do I love thee? Let me count the ways.
I love thee to the depth and breadth and height
My soul can reach, when feeling out of sight
For the ends of Being and ideal Grace.
5   I love thee to the level of every day's
Most quiet need, by sun and candle-light.
I love thee freely, as men strive for Right;
I love thee purely, as they turn from Praise.
I love thee with the passion put to use
10   In my old griefs, and with my childhood's faith.
I love thee with a love I seemed to lose
With my lost saints, – I love thee with the breath,
Smiles, tears, of all my life! – and, if God choose,
I shall but love thee better after death.

Elizabeth Barrett Browning

Elizabeth Barrett Browning

My Last Duchess

That's my last Duchess painted on the wall,
Looking as if she were alive; I call
That piece a wonder, now: Frà Pandolf's hands
Worked busily a day, and there she stands.
5　Will't please you sit and look at her? I said
'Frà Pandolf' by design, for never read
Strangers like you that pictured countenance,
The depth and passion of its earnest glance,
But to myself they turned (since none puts by
10　The curtain I have drawn for you, but I)
And seemed as they would ask me, if they durst,
How such a glance came there; so, not the first
Are you to turn and ask thus. Sir, 'twas not
Her husband's presence only, called that spot
15　Of joy into the Duchess' cheek: perhaps
Frà Pandolf chanced to say 'Her mantle laps
'Over my Lady's wrist too much,' or 'Paint
'Must never hope to reproduce the faint
'Half-flush that dies along her throat;' such stuff
20　Was courtesy, she thought, and cause enough
For calling up that spot of joy. She had
A heart...how shall I say?...too soon made glad,
Too easily impressed; she liked whate'er
She looked on, and her looks went everywhere.
25　Sir, 'twas all one! My favour at her breast,
The dropping of the daylight in the West,
The bough of cherries some officious fool
Broke in the orchard for her, the white mule
She rode with round the terrace – all and each
30　Would draw from her alike the approving speech,
Or blush, at least. She thanked men, – good; but thanked
Somehow...I know not how...as if she ranked
My gift of a nine hundred years old name
With anybody's gift. Who'd stoop to blame
35　This sort of trifling? Even had you skill
In speech – (which I have not) – to make your will
Quite clear to such an one, and say 'Just this
'Or that in you disgusts me; here you miss,
'Or there exceed the mark' – and if she let
40　Herself be lessoned so, nor plainly set
Her wits to yours, forsooth, and made excuse,
– E'en then would be some stooping, and I chuse
Never to stoop. Oh, Sir, she smiled, no doubt,
Whene'er I passed her; but who passed without
45　Much the same smile? This grew; I gave commands;

Then all smiles stopped together. There she stands
As if alive. Will't please you rise? we'll meet
The company below, then. I repeat,
The Count your Master's known munificence
50 Is ample warrant that no just pretence
Of mine for dowry will be disallowed;
Though his fair daughter's self, as I avowed
At starting, is my object. Nay, we'll go
Together down, Sir! Notice Neptune, tho',
55 Taming a sea-horse, thought a rarity,
Which Claus of Innsbruck cast in bronze for me.

Robert Browning

Ulysses

It little profits that an idle king,
By this still hearth, among these barren crags,
Matched with an aged wife, I mete and dole
Unequal laws unto a savage race,
5 That hoard, and sleep, and feed, and know not me.
I cannot rest from travel; I will drink
Life to the lees. All times I have enjoyed
Greatly, have suffered greatly, both with those
That loved me, and alone; on shore, and when
10 Through scudding drifts the rainy Hyades
Vext the dim sea. I am become a name;
For always roaming with a hungry heart
Much have I seen and known – cities of men
And manners, climates, councils, governments,
15 Myself not least, but honoured of them all, –
And drunk delight of battle with my peers,
Far on the ringing plains of windy Troy.
I am a part of all that I have met;
Yet all experience is an arch wherethrough
20 Gleams that untravelled world whose margin fades
For ever and for ever when I move.
How dull it is to pause, to make an end,
To rust unburnished, not to shine in use!
As though to breathe were life! Life piled on life
25 Were all too little, and of one to me
Little remains; but every hour is saved
From that eternal silence, something more,
A bringer of new things; and vile it were
For some three suns to store and hoard myself,
30 And this grey spirit yearning in desire

To follow knowledge like a sinking star,
Beyond the utmost bound of human thought.
    This is my son, mine own Telemachus,
To whom I leave the sceptre and the isle,
35 Well-loved of me, discerning to fulfil
This labour, by slow prudence to make mild
A rugged people, and through soft degrees
Subdue them to the useful and the good.
Most blameless is he, centred in the sphere
40 Of common duties, decent not to fail
In offices of tenderness, and pay
Meet adoration to my household gods,
When I am gone. He works his work, I mine.
    There lies the port; the vessel puffs her sail;
45 There gloom the dark, broad seas. My mariners,
Souls that have toiled, and wrought, and thought with me,
That ever with a frolic welcome took
The thunder and the sunshine, and opposed
Free hearts, free foreheads – you and I are old;
50 Old age hath yet his honour and his toil.
Death closes all; but something ere the end,
Some work of noble note, may yet be done,
Not unbecoming men that strove with gods.
The lights begin to twinkle from the rocks;
55 The long day wanes; the slow moon climbs; the deep
Moans round with many voices. Come, my friends,
'Tis not too late to seek a newer world.
Push off, and sitting well in order smite
The sounding furrows; for my purpose holds
60 To sail beyond the sunset, and the baths
Of all the western stars, until I die.
It may be that the gulfs will wash us down;
It may be we shall touch the Happy Isles,
And see the great Archilles, whom we knew.
65 Though much is taken, much abides; and though
We are not now that strength which in old days
Moved earth and heaven, that which we are, we are,
One equal temper of heroic hearts,
Made weak by time and fate, but strong in will
70 To strive, to seek, to find, and not to yield.

Alfred, Lord Tennyson

Remember

Remember me when I am gone away,
    Gone far away into the silent land;
    When you can no more hold me by the hand,
Nor I half turn to go yet turning stay.
5 Remember me when no more day by day
    You tell me of our future that you planned:
    Only remember me; you understand
It will be late to counsel then or pray.
Yet if you should forget me for a while
10   And afterwards remember, do not grieve:
    For if the darkness and corruption leave
    A vestige of the thoughts that once I had,
Better by far you should forget and smile
    Than that you should remember and be sad.

Christina Rossetti

God's Grandeur

The world is charged with the grandeur of God.
    It will flame out, like shining from shook foil;
    It gathers to a greatness, like the ooze of oil
Crushed. Why do men then now not reck his rod?
5 Generations have trod, have trod, have trod;
    And all is seared with trade; bleared, smeared with toil;
    And wears man's smudge and shares man's smell: the soil
Is bare now, nor can foot feel, being shod.

And for all this, nature is never spent;
10   There lives the dearest freshness deep down things;
And though the last lights off the black West went
    Oh, morning, at the brown brink eastward, springs –
Because the Holy Ghost over the bent
    World broods with warm breast and with ah! bright wings.

Gerard Manley Hopkins

1900 – 1950

The Darkling Thrush

I leant upon a coppice gate
    When Frost was spectre-grey,
And Winter's dregs made desolate
    The weakening eye of day.
The tangled bine-stems scored the sky
5   Like strings of broken lyres,
And all mankind that haunted nigh
    Had sought their household fires.

The land's sharp features seemed to be
    The Century's corpse outleant,
10 His crypt the cloudy canopy,
    The wind his death-lament.
The ancient pulse of germ and birth
    Was shrunken hard and dry,
And every spirit upon earth
15   Seemed fervourless as I.

At once a voice arose among
    The bleak twigs overhead
In a full-hearted evensong
    Of joy illimited;
20 An aged thrush, frail, gaunt, and small,
    In blast-beruffled plume,
Had chosen thus to fling his soul
    Upon the growing gloom.

So little cause for carolings
25   Of such ecstatic sound
Was written on terrestrial things
    Afar or nigh around,
That I could think there trembled through
    His happy good-night air
30 Some blessed Hope, whereof he knew
    And I was unaware.

Thomas Hardy

The Way Through the Woods

They shut the road through the woods
Seventy years ago.
Weather and rain have undone it again,
And now you would never know
5   There was once a road through the woods
Before they planted the trees.

It is underneath the coppice and heath
And the thin anemones.
Only the keeper sees
10   That, where the ring-dove broods,
And the badgers roll at ease,
There was once a road through the woods.

Yet, if you enter the woods
Of a summer evening late,
15   When the night-air cools on the trout-ringed pools
Where the otter whistles his mate,
(They fear not men in the woods,
Because they see so few.)
You will hear the beat of a horse's feet,
20   And the swish of a skirt in the dew,
Steadily cantering through
The misty solitudes,
As though they perfectly knew
The old lost road through the woods...
25   But there is no road through the woods.

Rudyard Kipling

The Love Song of J. Alfred Prufrock

S'io credesse che mia risposta fosse
A persona che mai tornasse al mondo,
Questa fiamma staria senza più scosse.
Ma per cìo che giammai di questo fondo
5 *Non tornò viva alcun, s'i'odo il vero,*
Senza tema d'infamia ti rispondo.

Let us go then, you and I,
When the evening is spread out against the sky
Like a patient etherized upon a table;
10 Let us go, through certain half-deserted streets,
The muttering retreats
Of restless nights in one-night cheap hotels
And sawdust restaurants with oyster-shells:
Streets that follow like a tedious argument
15 Of insidious intent
To lead you to an overwhelming question...
Oh, do not ask, "What is it?"
Let us go and make our visit.

In the room the women come and go
20 Talking of Michelangelo.

The yellow fog that rubs its back upon the window-panes,
The yellow smoke that rubs its muzzle on the window-panes
Licked its tongue into the corners of the evening,
Lingered upon the pools that stand in drains,
25 Let fall upon its back the soot that falls from chimneys,
Slipped by the terrace, made a sudden leap,
And seeing that it was a soft October night,
Curled once about the house, and fell asleep.

And indeed there will be time
30 For the yellow smoke that slides along the street
Rubbing its back upon the window-panes;
There will be time, there will be time
To prepare a face to meet the faces that you meet;
There will be time to murder and create,
35 And time for all the works and days of hands
That lift and drop a question on your plate;
Time for you and time for me,
And time yet for a hundred indecisions,
And for a hundred visions and revisions,
40 Before the taking of a toast and tea.

In the room the women come and go
Talking of Michelangelo.

And indeed there will be time
To wonder, "Do I dare?" and, "Do I dare?"
45 Time to turn back and descend the stair,
With a bald spot in the middle of my hair –
[They will say: "How his hair is growing thin!"]
My morning coat, my collar mounting firmly to the chin,
My necktie rich and modest, but asserted by a simple pin –
50 [They will say: "But how his arms and legs are thin!"]
Do I dare
Disturb the universe?
In a minute there is time
For decisions and revisions which a minute will reverse.

55 For I have known them all already, known them all –
Have known the evenings, mornings, afternoons,
I have measured out my life with coffee spoons;
I know the voices dying with a dying fall
Beneath the music from a farther room.
60 So how should I presume?

And I have known the eyes already, known them all –
The eyes that fix you in a formulated phrase,
And when I am formulated, sprawling on a pin,
When I am pinned and wriggling on the wall,
65 Then how should I begin
To spit out all the butt-ends of my days and ways?
    And how should I presume?

And I have known the arms already, known them all –
Arms that are braceleted and white and bare
70 [But in the lamplight, downed with light brown hair!]
Is it perfume from a dress
That makes me so digress?
Arms that lie along a table, or wrap about a shawl.
    And should I then presume?
75   And how should I begin?

Shall I say, I have gone at dusk through narrow streets
And watched the smoke that rises from the pipes
Of lonely men in shirt-sleeves, leaning out of windows?...

    I should have been a pair of ragged claws
80 Scuttling across the floors of silent seas.

And the afternoon, the evening, sleeps so peacefully!
Smoothed by long fingers,
Asleep...tired...or it malingers,

Stretched on the floor, here beside you and me.
85 Should I, after tea and cakes and ices,
Have the strength to force the moment to its crisis?
But though I have wept and fasted, wept and prayed,
Though I have seen my head [grown slightly bald] brought in upon a platter,
I am no prophet – and here's no great matter;
90 I have seen the moment of my greatness flicker,
And I have seen the eternal Footman hold my coat, and snicker,
And in short, I was afraid.

And would it have been worth it, after all,
After the cups, the marmalade, the tea,
95 Among the porcelain, among some talk of you and me,
Would it have been worth while,
To have bitten off the matter with a smile,
To have squeezed the universe into a ball
To roll it toward some overwhelming question,
100 To say: "I am Lazarus, come from the dead,
Come back to tell you all, I shall tell you all"–
If one, settling a pillow by her head,
        Should say: "That is not what I meant at all.
        That is not it, at all."

105   And would it have been worth it, after all,
Would it have been worth while,
After the sunsets and the dooryards and the sprinkled streets,
After the novels, after the teacups, after the skirts that trail along the floor –
And this, and so much more? –
110 It is impossible to say just what I mean!
But as if a magic lantern threw the nerves in patterns on a screen:
Would it have been worth while
If one, settling a pillow or throwing off a shawl,
And turning toward the window, should say:
115   "That is not it at all,
        That is not what I meant, at all."

No! I am not Prince Hamlet, nor was meant to be;
Am an attendant lord, one that will do
To swell a progress, start a scene or two,
120 Advise the prince; no doubt, an easy tool,
Deferential, glad to be of use,
Politic, cautious, and meticulous;
Full of high sentence, but a bit obtuse;
At times, indeed, almost ridiculous –
125 Almost, at times, the Fool.

    I grow old…I grow old…
I shall wear the bottoms of my trousers rolled.

Shall I part my hair behind? Do I dare to eat a peach?
I shall wear white flannel trousers, and walk upon the beach.
130 I have heard the mermaids singing, each to each.

I do not think that they will sing to me.

I have seen them riding seaward on the waves
Combing the white hair of the waves blown back
When the wind blows the water white and black.

135 We have lingered in the chambers of the sea
By sea-girls wreathed with seaweed red and brown
Till human voices wake us, and we drown.

T.S. Eliot

The Second Coming

Turning and turning in the widening gyre
The falcon cannot hear the falconer;
Things fall apart; the centre cannot hold;
Mere anarchy is loosed upon the world,
5 The blood-dimmed tide is loosed, and everywhere
The ceremony of innocence is drowned;
The best lack all conviction, while the worst
Are full of passionate intensity.

Surely some revelation is at hand;
10 Surely the Second Coming is at hand.
The Second Coming! Hardly are those words out
When a vast image out of *Spiritus Mundi*
Troubles my sight: somewhere in sands of the desert
A shape with lion body and the head of a man,
15 A gaze blank and pitiless as the sun,
Is moving its slow thighs, while all about it
Reel shadows of the indignant desert birds.
The darkness drops again; but now I know
That twenty centuries of stony sleep
20 Were vexed to nightmare by a rocking cradle,
And what rough beast, its hour come round at last,
Slouches towards Bethlehem to be born?

W.B. Yeats

O What is That Sound

O what is that sound which so thrills the ear
    Down in the valley drumming, drumming?
Only the scarlet soldiers, dear,
    The soldiers coming.

5 O what is that light I see flashing so clear
    Over the distance brightly, brightly?
Only the sun on their weapons, dear,
    As they step lightly.

O what are they doing with all that gear,
10   What are they doing this morning, this morning?
Only their usual manoeuvres, dear,
    Or perhaps a warning.

O why have they left the road down there,
    Why are they suddenly wheeling, wheeling?
15 Perhaps a change in their orders, dear.
    Why are you kneeling?

O haven't they stopped for the doctor's care,
    Haven't they reined their horses, their horses?
Why, they are none of them wounded, dear,
20   None of these forces.

O is it the parson they want, with white hair,
    Is it the parson, is it, is it?
No, they are passing his gateway, dear,
    Without a visit.

25 O it must be the farmer who lives so near.
    It must be the farmer so cunning, so cunning?
They have passed the farmyard already, dear,
    And now they are running.

O where are you going? Stay with me here!
30   Were the vows you swore deceiving, deceiving?
No, I promised to love you, dear,
    But I must be leaving.

O it's broken the lock and splintered the door,
    O it's the gate where they're turning, turning;
35 Their boots are heavy on the floor
    And their eyes are burning.

W.H. Auden

Prayer Before Birth

I am not yet born; O hear me.
Let not the bloodsucking bat or the rat or the stoat or the
     club-footed ghoul come near me.

I am not yet born, console me.
5 I fear that the human race may with tall walls wall me,
     with strong drugs dope me, with wise lies lure me,
       on black racks rack me, in blood-baths roll me.

I am not yet born; provide me
With water to dandle me, grass to grow for me, trees to talk
10   to me, sky to sing to me, birds and a white light
       in the back of my mind to guide me.

I am not yet born; forgive me
For the sins that in me the world shall commit, my words
     when they speak me, my thoughts when they think me,
15   my treason engendered by traitors beyond me,
        my life, when they murder by means of my
         hands, my death when they live me.

I am not yet born; rehearse me
In the parts I must play and the cues I must take when
20   old men lecture me, bureaucrats hector me, mountains
       frown at me, lovers laugh at me, the white
        waves call me to folly and the desert calls
         me to doom and the beggar refuses
          my gift and my children curse me.

25 I am not yet born; O hear me,
Let not the man who is beast or who thinks he is God
     come near me.

I am not yet born; O fill me
With strength against those who would freeze my
30   humanity, would dragoon me into a lethal automaton,
       would make me a cog in a machine, a thing with
        one face, a thing, and against all those
         who would dissipate my entirety, would
          blow me like thistledown hither and
35   thither or hither and thither
            like water held in the
             hands would spill me.

Let them not make me a stone and let them not spill me.
Otherwise kill me.

Louis MacNeice

26

Do Not Go Gentle Into That Good Night

Do not go gentle into that good night,
Old age should burn and rave at close of day;
Rage, rage against the dying of the light.

Though wise men at their end know dark is right,
5 Because their words had forked no lightning they
Do not go gentle into that good night.

Good men, the last wave by, crying how bright
Their frail deeds might have danced in a green bay,
Rage, rage against the dying of the light.

10 Wild men who caught and sang the sun in flight,
And learn, too late, they grieved it on its way,
Do not go gentle into that good night.

Grave men, near death, who see with blinding sight
Blind eyes could blaze like meteors and be gay,
15 Rage, rage against the dying of the light.

And you, my father, there on the sad height,
Curse, bless, me now with your fierce tears, I pray.
Do not go gentle into that good night.
Rage, rage against the dying of the light.

Dylan Thomas

Dylan Thomas

Easter Monday

(In Memoriam E. T.)

In the last letter that I had from France
You thanked me for the silver Easter egg
Which I had hidden in the box of apples
You liked to munch beyond all other fruit.
5   You found the egg the Monday before Easter,
And said, 'I will praise Easter Monday now –
It was such a lovely morning.' Then you spoke
Of the coming battle and said, 'This is the eve.
Good-bye. And may I have a letter soon.'

10   That Easter Monday was a day for praise,
It was such a lovely morning. In our garden
We sowed our earliest seeds, and in the orchard
The apple-bud was ripe. It was the eve.
There are three letters that you will not get.

April 9th, 1917

Eleanor Farjeon

Here

I am a man now.
Pass your hand over my brow,
You can feel the place where the brains grow.

I am like a tree,
5   From my top boughs I can see
The footprints that led up to me.

There is blood in my veins
That has run clear of the stain
Contracted in so many loins.

10   Why, then, are my hands red
With the blood of so many dead?
Is this where I was misled?

Why are my hands this way
That they will not do as I say?
15   Does no God hear when I pray?

I have nowhere to go.
The swift satellites show
The clock of my whole being is slow.

It is too late to start
20   For destinations not of the heart.
I must stay here with my hurt.

R.S. Thomas

Abbey Tomb

I told them not to ring the bells
The night the Vikings came
Out of the sea and passed us by.
The fog was thick as cream
5   And in the abbey we stood still
As if our breath might blare
Or pulses rattle if we once
Stopped staring at the door.

Through the walls and through the fog
10   We heard them passing by.
The deafer monks thanked God too soon
And later only I
Could catch the sound of prowling men
Still present in the hills
15   So everybody else agreed
To ring the abbey bells.

And even while the final clang
Still snored upon the air,
And while the ringers joked their way
20   Down round the spiral stair,
Before the spit of fervent prayer
Had dried into the stone
The raiders came back through the fog
And killed us one by one.

25   Father Abbot at the altar
Lay back with his knees
Doubled under him, caught napping
In the act of praise.
Brother John lay unresponsive
30   In the warming room.
The spiders came out for the heat
And then the rats for him.

Under the level of the sheep
Who graze here all the time
35   We lie now, under tourists' feet
Who in good weather come.
I told them not to ring the bells,
But centuries of rain
And blustering have made their tombs
40   Look just as right as mine.

Patricia Beer

An Arundel Tomb

Side by side, their faces blurred,
The earl and countess lie in stone,
Their proper habits vaguely shown
As jointed armour, stiffened pleat,
5 And that faint hint of the absurd –
The little dogs under their feet.

Such plainness of the pre-baroque
Hardly involves the eye, until
It meets his left-hand gauntlet, still
10 Clasped empty in the other; and
One sees, with a sharp tender shock,
His hand withdrawn, holding her hand.

They would not think to lie so long.
Such faithfulness in effigy
15 Was just a detail friends would see:
A sculptor's sweet commissioned grace
Thrown off in helping to prolong
The Latin names around the base.

They would not guess how early in
20 Their supine stationary voyage
The air would change to soundless damage,
Turn the old tenantry away;
How soon succeeding eyes begin
To look, not read. Rigidly they

25 Persisted, linked, through lengths and breadths
Of time. Snow fell, undated. Light
Each summer thronged the glass. A bright
Litter of birdcalls strewed the same
Bone-riddled ground. And up the paths
30 The endless altered people came,

Washing at their identity.
Now, helpless in the hollow of
An unarmorial age, a trough
Of smoke in slow suspended skeins
35 Above their scrap of history,
Only an attitude remains:

Time has transfigured them into
Untruth. The stone fidelity
They hardly meant has come to be
40 Their final blazon, and to prove
Our almost-instinct almost true:
What will survive of us is love.

Philip Larkin

Wuthering Heights

Walter was guide. His mother's cousin
Inherited some Brontë soup dishes.
He felt sorry for them. Writers
Were pathetic people. Hiding from it
5   And making it up. But your transatlantic elation
Elated him. He effervesced
Like his rhubarb wine kept a bit too long:
A vintage of legends and gossip
About those poor lasses. Then,
10 After the Rectory, after the chaise longue
Where Emily died, and the midget hand-made books,
The elvish lacework, the dwarfish fairy-work shoes,
It was the track for Stanbury. That climb
A mile beyond expectation, into
15 Emily's private Eden. The moor
Lifted and opened its dark flower
For you too. That was satisfactory.
Wilder, maybe, than ever Emily knew it,
With wet feet and nothing on her head
20 She trudged that climbing side towards friends
Probably. Dark redoubt
On the skyline above. It was all
Novel and exhilarating to you.
The book becoming a map. *Wuthering Heights*
25 Withering into perspective. We got there
And it was all gaze. The open moor,
Gamma rays and decomposing starlight
Had repossessed it
With a kind of blackening smoulder. The centuries
30 Of door-bolted comfort finally amounted
To a forsaken quarry. The roofs'
Deadfall slabs were flaking, but mostly in place,
Beam and purlins softening. So hard
To imagine the life that had lit
35 Such a sodden, raw-stone cramp of refuge.
The floors were a rubble of stone and sheep droppings.
Doorframes, windowframes –
Gone to make picnickers' fires or evaporated.
Only the stonework – black. The sky – blue.
40 And the moor-wind flickering.
                              The incomings,
The outgoings – how would you take up now
The clench of that struggle? The leakage
Of earnings off a few sickly bullocks
And a scatter of crazed sheep. Being cornered
45 Kept folk here. Was that crumble of wall
Remembering a try at a garden? Two trees
Planted for company, for a child to play under,

And to have something to stare at. Sycamores –
The girth and spread of valley twenty-year-olds,
50 They were probably ninety.
                                        You breathed it all in
With jealous, emulous snifflings. Weren't you
Twice as ambitious as Emily? Odd
To watch you, such a brisk pendant
Of your globe-circling aspirations.
55 Among those burned-out, worn-out remains
Of failed efforts, failed hopes –
Iron beliefs, iron necessities,
Iron bondage, already
Crumbling back to the wild stone.
                                        You perched
60 In one of the two trees
Just where the snapshot shows you.
Doing as Emily never did. You
Had all the liberties, having life.
The future had invested in you –
65 As you might say of a jewel
So brilliantly faceted, refracting
Every tint, where Emily had stared
Like a dying prisoner.
And a poem unfurled from you
70 Like a loose frond of hair from your nape
To be clipped and kept in a book. What would stern
Dour Emily have made of your frisky glances
And your huge hope? Your huge
Mortgage of hope. The moor-wind
75 Came with its empty eyes to look at you.
And the clouds gazed sidelong, going elsewhere,
The heath-grass, fidgeting in its fever,
Took idiot notice of you. And the stone,
Reaching to touch your hand, found you real
80 And warm, and lucent, like that earlier one.
And maybe a ghost, trying to hear your words,
Peered from the broken mullions
And was stilled. Or was suddenly aflame
With the scorch of doubled envy. Only
85 Gradually quenched in understanding.

Ted Hughes

Wuthering Heights

The horizons ring me like faggots,
Tilted and disparate, and always unstable.
Touched by a match, they might warm me,
And their fine lines singe
5   The air to orange
Before the distances they pin evaporate,
Weighting the pale sky with a solider colour.
But they only dissolve and dissolve
Like a series of promises, as I step forward.

10   There is no life higher than the grasstops
Or the hearts of sheep, and the wind
Pours by like destiny, bending
Everything in one direction.
I can feel it trying
15   To funnel my heat away.
If I pay the roots of the heather
Too close attention, they will invite me
To whiten my bones among them.

The sheep know where they are,
20   Browsing in their dirty wool-clouds,
Grey as the weather.
The black slots of their pupils take me in.
It is like being mailed into space,
A thin, silly message.
25   They stand about in grandmotherly disguise,
All wig curls and yellow teeth
And hard, marbly baas.

I come to wheel ruts, and water
Limpid as the solitudes
30   That flee through my fingers.
Hollow doorsteps go from grass to grass;
Lintel and sill have unhinged themselves.
Of people the air only
Remembers a few odd syllables.
35   It rehearses them moaningly:
Black stone, black stone.

The sky leans on me, me, the one upright
Among all horizontals.
The grass is beating its head distractedly.
40   It is too delicate
For a life in such company;
Darkness terrifies it.
Now, in valleys narrow
And black as purses, the house lights
45   Gleam like small change.

Sylvia Plath

All the Things You Are Not Yet

for Tess

Tonight there's a crowd in my head:
all the things you are not yet.
You are words without paper, pages
sighing in summer forests, gardens
5   where builders stub out their rubble
and plastic oozes its sweat.
All the things you are, you are not yet.

Not yet the lonely window in midwinter
with the whine of tea on an empty stomach,
10   not yet the heating you can't afford and must wait for,
tamping a coin in on each hour.
Not the gorgeous shush of restaurant doors
and their interiors, always so much smaller.
Not the smell of the newsprint, the blur
15   on your fingertips – your fame. Not yet

the love you will have for Winter Pearmains
and Chanel No 5 – and then your being unable
to buy both washing-machine and computer
when your baby's due to be born,
20   and my voice saying, 'I'll get you one'
and you frowning, frowning
at walls and surfaces which are not mine –
all this, not yet. Give me your hand,

that small one without a mark of work on it,
25   the one that's strange to the washing-up bowl
and doesn't know Fairy Liquid from whiskey.
Not yet the moment of your arrival in taxis
at daring destinations, or your being alone at stations
with the skirts of your fashionable clothes flapping
30   and no money for the telephone.

Not yet the moment when I can give you nothing
so well-folded it fits in an envelope –
a dull letter you won't reread.
Not yet the moment of your assimilation
35   in that river flowing westward: rivers of clothes,
of dreams, an accent unlike my own
saying to someone I don't know: *darling...*

Helen Dunmore

Marged

I think of her sometimes when I lie in bed,
falling asleep in the room I have made in the roof-space
over the old dark parlŵr where she died
alone in winter, ill and penniless.
5 Lighting the lamps, November afternoons,
a reading book, whisky gold in my glass.
At my type-writer tapping under stars
at my new roof-window, radio tunes
and dog for company. Or parking the car
10 where through the mud she called her single cow
up from the field, under the sycamore.
Or looking at the hills she looked at too.
I find her broken crocks, digging her garden.
What else do we share, but being women?

Gillian Clarke

Gillian Clarke

Poetry Around the World

This is a Photograph of Me

It was taken some time ago.
At first it seems to be
a smeared
print: blurred lines and grey flecks
5 blended with the paper;

then, as you scan

it, you see in the left-hand corner
a thing that is like a branch: part of a tree
(balsam or spruce) emerging
10 and, to the right, halfway up
what ought to be a gentle
slope, a small frame house.

In the background there is a lake,
and beyond that, some low hills.

15 (The photograph was taken
the day after I drowned.

I am in the lake, in the centre
of the picture, just under the surface.

It is difficult to say where
20 precisely, or to say
how large or small I am:
the effect of water
on light is a distortion

but if you look long enough,
25 eventually
you will be able to see me.)

Margaret Atwood

This is a Photograph of Me

Oddjob, a Bull Terrier

You prepare for one sorrow,
but another comes.
It is not like the weather,
you cannot brace yourself,
5   the unreadiness is all.
Your companion, the woman,
the friend next to you,
the child at your side,
and the dog,
10   we tremble for them,
we look seaward and muse
it will rain.
We shall get ready for rain;
you do not connect
15   the sunlight altering
the darkening oleanders
in the sea-garden,
the gold going out of the palms.
You do not connect this,
20   the fleck of the drizzle
on your flesh
with the dog's whimper,
the thunder doesn't frighten,
the readiness is all;
25   what follows your feet
is trying to tell you
the silence is all;
it is deeper than the readiness,
it is sea-deep,
30   earth-deep,
love-deep.

The silence
is stronger than thunder,
we are stricken dumb and deep
35   as the animals who never utter love
as we do, except
it becomes unutterable
and must be said,
in a whimper,
40   in tears,
in the drizzle that comes to our eyes
not uttering the loved thing's name,
the silence of the dead,
the silence of the deepest buried love is
45   the one silence,
and whether we bear it for beast,
for child, for woman, or friend,
it is the one love, it is the same,
and it is blest
50   deepest by loss
it is blest, it is blest.

Derek Walcott

Iguana Memory

Saw an iguana once
when I was very small
in our backdam backyard
came rustling across my path

5 green like moving newleaf sunlight

big like big big lizard
with more legs than centipede
so it seemed to me
and it must have stopped a while
10 eyes meeting mine
iguana and child locked in a brief
split moment happening
before it went hurrying

    for the green of its life

Grace Nichols

Grace Nichols

New Zealand

(For Monte Holcroft)

These unshaped islands, on the sawyer's bench,
Wait for the chisel of the mind,
Green canyons to the south, immense and passive,
Penetrated rarely, seeded only
5 By the deer-culler's shot, or else in the north
Tribes of the shark and the octopus,
Mangroves, black hair on a boxer's hand.

The founding fathers with their guns and bibles,
Botanist, whaler, added bones and names
10 To the land, to us a bridle
As if the id were a horse: the swampy towns
Like dreamers that struggle to wake,

Longing for the poet's truth
And the lover's pride. Something new and old
15 Explores its own pain, hearing

The rain's choir on curtains of grey moss
Or fingers of the Tasman pressing
On breasts of hardening sand, as actors
Find their own solitude in mirrors,

20 As one who has buried his dead,
Able at last to give with an open hand.

James K. Baxter

Trees at the Arctic Circle

(SALIX CORDIFOLIA–GROUND WILLOW)

They are 18 inches long
or even less
crawling under rocks
groveling among the lichens
5 bending and curling to escape
making themselves small
finding new ways to hide
Coward trees
I am angry to see them
10 like this
not proud of what they are
bowing to weather instead
careful of themselves
worried about the sky
15 afraid of exposing their limbs
like a Victorian married couple

I call to mind great Douglas firs
I see tall maples waving green
and oaks like gods in autumn gold
20 the whole horizon jungle dark
and I crouched under that continual light
But these
even the dwarf shrubs of Ontario
mock them
25 Coward trees

And yet – and yet –
their seed pods glow
like delicate grey earrings
their leaves are veined and intricate

30 like tiny parkas
They have about three months
to make sure the species does not die
and that's how they spend their time
unbothered by any human opinion
35 just digging in here and now
sending their roots down down down
And you know it occurs to me
    about 2 feet under
those roots must touch permafrost

40 ice that remains ice forever
and they use it for their nourishment
they use death to remain alive

I see that I've been carried away
in my scorn of the dwarf trees
45 most foolish in my judgments
To take away the dignity
    of any living thing
even tho it cannot understand
    the scornful words
50 is to make life itself trivial
and yourself the Pontifex Maximus[1]
    of nullity
I have been stupid in a poem
I will not alter the poem
55 but let the stupidity remain permanent
as the trees are
in a poem
the dwarf trees of Baffin Island
Pangnirtung[2]

Al Purdy

1. Chief priest.
2. The largest island of the Canadian Arctic.
   Pangnirtung is a trading post in eastern Baffin Island, just south of the Arctic Circle.

Callaloo

Mix up
like callaloo[1]
Not no watery callaloo
But
5 a thick, hot, sweet
callaloo
burnin' you tongue
Wid dem chunk o' dumplin'
goin' down nice
10 an' wid coconut
wid o' widdout deaders
as de case may be
as de taste may be
as de pocket may be
15 but sweet
an' hot

Dat is what it feel like
to be part o' dis
Revolution reality
20 O' dis
wakin' up reality
o' dis
no more hidin' you passport
reality
25 no more
hangin' you head
an' shufflin' you foot
an' tryin' to hide
behin' de person
30 in front o' you
like little Janet
behin' she mudder skirt

when de man ask
'whey you from?'

35 No more
playin' you doh hear
or sayin' some shit like
A...a...a...island
near by Trinidad
40 Or
a...a few mile
off Venezuela
but out loud an' bole

like you make de name
45 GRENADA!

An' wid you head in de air
becus de world is yours
an' you know is yours
an' you not goin' be
50 meek
meek
meek
an' wait to see
if
55 somebody
goin' let you
inherit the earth
becus you know arready
is yours

60 so you say
loud
an' clear
an' proud
GRENADA!
65 an' you silent scream
which he musbe hear
becus he look up
into your claimin' eyes
says
70 Dat mean Revolution
Dat mean Progress
Dat mean Forward!
Dat mean
sharin'
75 an' carin'
an' believin'
an' livin'
an' lovin'

Dat mean
80 a country in the Caribbean
in Latin America
in the Americas
in the struggle
in the world

1. Popular soup made from the leaf of the dasheen plant.

85 Dat mean, Comrade
a people
like de people
in Cuba
in Nicaragua
90 In Zimbabwe
in Mozambique
in strugglin' South Africa
in all dem countries
whey de people know
95 dat doh donkey say
de worl' ain't level
even donkey heself
musbe does shake he head
to feel dem bumps
100 an' know

how t'ing so hard
for some toc
an' so sof'
for others

105 All o' we
in all o' dis worl'
so mix up
like callaloo

an' yet
110 so not like callaloo
an' dat is why
de change
an' de promise
of de change
115 is sweet an' strong
like de soup
w'en Grannie
cover it down dey
an' let it
120 consomme
like dat
hot
sweet
burnin'
125 heavy
heavy

ca-lla-loo!

Merle Collins

42

Maninagar Days

They are always there
just as pigeons or flies
can be *always there*
and the children have to fight them off,
5 especially during those hot May afternoons
when they dare to jump down from the trees
into the cool shaded spots, the corners between
the canna flower beds
still moist from the morning's watering.

10 Monkeys in the garden –
I'm talking about rhesus monkeys
the colour of dirt roads and khaki
    and sometimes even of honey.
Rhesus monkeys that travel in small groups,

15 They are lean twirls, strong tails, fast shadows
abrupt with yellow teeth.
The monkeys are not so innocent
the elders warn,
not so content with their daily routine
20 for they are turning
into urban thieves, imitating
and even outdoing the crows:

One day a tall monkey leaped down on the clothesline
and stole a blinding white shirt.
25 Another day, a very muscular monkey
bounded out of the neighbour's house
with a huge rock of golden *gur*, solid raw sugar.
The boy was impressed. His mother
would have difficulty carrying such a load.

30 Still, the children treat the monkeys
as if they were children newly arrived from a foreign
country, unable to speak the language yet.

And the children's grandmother comes out
to the front door from time to time.
35 Just awakened from her afternoon nap, now
she readjusts her thin white sari
and squints against the sun
watching over them all –
And the faint May breeze that struggles
40 through the monkey crowded branches
is Hanuman's breath.
How could you know it, how could you miss it
unless you had lived
in such a garden.

45 Monkeys in the garden.
They are always there,
usually in the gulmuhore trees
chewing on the sour rubbery leaves
and the even more delicious bright
50 scarlet-orange flowers: petals
sparkling as sliced blood oranges,
water-plump green stems...

The monkeys have become everything
to the children, although
55 the children are not aware of it yet,
and one summer the children can't help
learning everything from them:
their noise, their shadows, their defiant stare,
the way they shake their heads,
60 the curve of their elbows,
their weight on the trees...
In fact, without the monkeys
the trees begin to look a little barren
to the children.

65 Oh there are days when the monkeys refuse
to come down from the gulmuhore trees
and that makes the children jealous
and unhappy.
Oh there are days when the monkeys
70 never intrude, never interfere
with the children's favourite hide-outs.
Peaceful days, one would think,
with the monkeys chatter-reclining and nibbling,
dozing and basking, jabbering and
75 lice-picking safe above in the gulmuhore trees
while the children run about exhausting
one game after another right below.
Peaceful hours, one would think.
But the children are jealous
80 for they too love to eat
the gulmuhore flowers and leaves.

Invariably they try
to convince the monkeys to throw some flowers down
and then, that failing,
85 invariably they try to persuade the monkeys
to come down into their garden
(maybe with some flowers)
and then, that failing,
they are simply angry, so angry
90 at the monkeys, they terrify them off

43

into the neighbouring gardens.
Oh with monkeys like that
the children believe in Hanuman.
In their secret wishes the children reinvent
95 the perfect monkey: Hanuman,
wild and fierce and loyal and gentle...

One day the boy defended his sisters
single-handedly with a stick like a sword
he chased the whole band of monkeys
100 not up the trees but to the back of the house:
a complete disappearance.
Then there was such silence

the girls were afraid – where
had all the birds gone? And the neighbour's dog?
105 A few minutes later the boy returned
running, chased by the monkeys,
and the stick like a sword was in the hand
of the angry leader...

Monkeys in the garden.
110 Some people have monkeys
in their dreams, monkeys in their nightmares,
monkeys crossing their shadows,
long after they have stopped being children,
long after they have left such a garden.

Sujata Bhatt

Hanuman is the son of the wind god Maruti and Anjana, a goddess turned into a monkey by a curse. Hanuman is the most powerful, most intelligent and most learned of the monkeys. He is also considered to be the 'Ideal of the perfect servant: A servant who finds full realisation of manhood, of faithfulness, of obedience. The subject whose glory is in his own inferiority' (P. Thomas: *Epics, Myths and Legends of India*). This ideal servant–master relationship is especially evident in Hanuman's devotion to Ramachandra in the epic *Ramayana*.

Ballads

Sir Patrick Spens

The king sits in Dumferling town,
    Drinking the blude-reid wine:
"O whar will I get guid sailor,
    To sail this ship of mine?"

5 Up and spak an eldern knicht,
    Sat at the king's richt knee:
"Sir Patrick Spens is the best sailor
    That sails upon the sea."

The king has written a braid letter
10   And signed it wi' his hand,
And sent it to Sir Patrick Spens,
    Was walking on the sand.

The first line that Sir Patrick read,
    A loud lauch lauched he;
15 The next line that Sir Patrick read,
    The tear blinded his ee.

"O wha is this has done this deed,
    This ill deed done to me,
To send me out this time o' the year,
20   To sail upon the sea?

"Mak haste, mak haste, my mirry men all,
    Our guid ship sails the morn."
"O say na sae, my master dear,
    For I fear a deadly storm.

25 "Late, late yestre'en I saw the new moon
    Wi' the auld moon in hir arm,
And I fear, I fear, my dear master,
    That we will come to harm."

O our Scots nobles were richt laith
30   To weet their cork-heeled shoon,
But lang or a' the play were played
    Their hats they swam aboon.

O lang, lang may their ladies sit,
    Wi' their fans into their hand,
35 Or ere they see Sir Patrick Spens
    Come sailing to the land.

O lang, lang may the ladies stand
    Wi' their gold kems in their hair,
Waiting for their ain dear lords,
40   For they'll see them na mair.

Half o'er, half o'er to Aberdour
    It's fifty fadom deep.
And their lies guid Sir Patrick Spens
    Wi' the Scots lords at his feet.

Anon.

The Wife of Usher's Well

There lived a wife at Usher's Well,
    And a wealthy wife was she;
She had three stout and stalwart sons,
    And sent them o'er the sea.

5 They hadna been a week from her,
    A week but barely ane,
Whan word came to the carlin wife
    That her three sons were gane.

They hadna been a week from her,
10   A week but barely three,
Whan word came to the carlin wife
    That her sons she'd never see.

"I wish the wind may never cease,
    Nor fashes in the flood,
15 Till my three sons come hame to me,
    In earthly flesh and blood."

It fell about the Martinmass,
    When nights are lang and mirk,
The carlin wife's three sons came hame,
20   And their hats were o' the birk.

It neither grew in syke nor ditch,
    Nor yet in any sheugh;
But at the gates o' Paradise,
    That birk grew fair eneugh.

25 "Blow up the fire, my maidens,
    Bring water from the well;
For a' my house shall feast this night,
    Since my three sons are well."

And she has made to them a bed,
30   She's made it large and wide,
And she's ta'en her mantle her about,
    Sat down at the bed-side.

Up then crew the red, red cock,
    And up and crew the gray;
35 The eldest to the youngest said,
    " 'T is time we were away."

The cock he hadna crawed but once,
    And clapped his wings at a',
When the youngest to the eldest said,
40   "Brother, we must awa'.

"The cock doth craw, the day doth daw,
    The channerin' worm doth chide;
Gin we be missed out o' our place,
    A sair pain we maun bide.

45 "Fare ye weel, my mother dear!
    Fareweel to barn and byre!
And fare ye weel, the bonny lass,
    That kindles my mother's fire!"

Anon.

The Twa Corbies

As I was walking all alane,
I heard twa corbies make a mane;
The tane unto the t'other say,
"Where sall we gang and dine to-day?"

5 "In behint you auld fail dike,
I wot there lies a new slain knight;
And naebody kens that he lies there,
But his hawk, his hound, and lady fair.

"His hound is to the hunting gane,
10 His hawk to fetch the wild-fowl hame,
His lady's ta'en another mate,
So we may mak our dinner sweet.

"Ye'll sit on his white hause-bane,
And I'll pike out his bonny blue een;
15 Wi' ae lock o' his gowden hair
We'll theek our nest when it grows bare.

"Mony a one for him makes mane,
But nane sall ken where he is gane;
O'er his white banes, when they are bare,
20 The wind sall blaw for evermair."

Anon.

The Three Ravens

There were three ravens sat on a tree,
Down a down, hay down, hay down
There were three ravens sat on a tree,
With a down
5   There were three ravens sat on a tree
They were as black as they might be.
With a down derry, derry, derry, down, down.

The one of them said to his mate,
"Where shall we our breakfast take?"

10 "Down in yonder greene field,
There lies a knight slain under his shield.

"His hounds they lie down at his feet,
So well they can their master keep.

"His hawks they fly so eagerly,
15 There's no fowl dare him come nigh."

Down there comes a fallow doe,
As great with young as she might go.

She lift up his bloody head
And kissed his wounds that were so red.

20 She got him up upon her back
And carried him to earthen lake.

She buried him before the prime;
She was dead herself ere even-song time.

God send every gentleman
25 Such hawks, such hounds, and such a leman.

Anon.

Edward

"Why does your brand sae drap wi' bluid,
  Edward, Edward,
Why does your brand sae drap wi' bluid,
  And why sae sad gang ye, O?"
5 "O I ha'e killed my hawk sae guid,
  Mither, mither,
O I ha'e killed my hawk sae guid,
  And I had nae mair but he, O."

"Your hawke's bluid was never sae reid,
10   Edward, Edward,
Your hawke's bluid was never sae reid,
  My dear son I tell thee, O."
"O I ha'e killed my reid-roan steed,
  Mither, mither,
15 O I ha'e killed my reid-roan steed,
  That erst was sae fair and free, O."

"Your steed was auld, and ye ha'e gat mair,
  Edward, Edward,
Your steed was auld, and ye ha'e gat mair,
20   Some other dule ye dree, O."
"O I ha'e killed my fader dear,
  Mither, mither,
O I ha'e killed my fader dear,
  Alas, and wae is me, O!"

25 "And whatten penance wul ye dree for that,
  Edward, Edward?
And whatten penance wul ye dree for that,
  My dear son, now tell me O?"
"I'll set my feet in yonder boat,

30   Mither, mither,
I'll set my feet in yonder boat,
  And I'll fare over the sea, O."

"And what wul ye do wi' your towers and your ha',
  Edward, Edward?
35 And what wul ye do wi' your towers and your ha',
  That were sae fair to see, O?"
"I'll let them stand tul they down fa',
  Mither, mither,
I'll let them stand tul they down fa',
40   For here never mair maun I be, O."

"And what wul ye leave to your bairns and your wife
  Edward, Edward?
And what wul ye leave to your bairns and your wife,
  When ye gang over the sea, O?"
45 "The warlde's room, let them beg thrae life,
  Mither, mither,
The warlde's room, let them beg thrae life,
  For them never mair wul I see, O."

"And what wul ye leave to your ain mither dear,
50   Edward, Edward?
And what wul ye leave to your ain mither dear,
  My dear son, now tell me, O?"
"The curse of hell frae me sall ye bear,
  Mither, mither,
55 The curse of hell frae me sall ye bear,
  Sic counsels ye gave to me, O."

Anon.

Tudor and Elizabethan Verse

They Flee From Me

They flee from me, that sometime did me seek,
With naked foot stalking in my chamber.
I have seen them, gentle, tame, and meek,
That now are wild, and do not remember
5   That sometime they put themselves in danger
To take bread at my hand; and now they range,
Busily seeking with a continual change.

Thanked be Fortune it hath been otherwise,
Twenty times better; but once in special,
10   In thin array, after a pleasant guise,
When her loose gown from her shoulders did fall,
And she me caught in her arms long and small,
And therewith all sweetly did me kiss
And softly said, "Dear heart, how like you this?"

15   It was no dream, I lay broad waking.
But all is turned, thorough my gentleness,
Into a strange fashion of forsaking;
And I have leave to go, of her goodness,
And she also to use newfangleness.
20   But since that I so kindely am served,
I fain would know what she hath deserved.

Thomas Wyatt

Sonnets

73

That time of year thou mayst in me behold
When yellow leaves, or none, or few, do hang
Upon those boughs which shake against the cold,
Bare ruined choirs, where late the sweet birds sang.
5 In me thou see'st the twilight of such day,
As after sunset fadeth in the west;
Which by and by black night doth take away,
Death's second self, that seals up all in rest.
In me thou see'st the glowing of such fire,
10 That on the ashes of his youth doth lie,
As the deathbed whereon it must expire,
Consumed with that which it was nourished by.
This thou perceiv'st, which makes thy love more strong,
To love that well, which thou must leave ere long.

116

Let me not to the marriage of true minds
Admit impediments. Love is not love
Which alters when it alteration finds,
Or bends with the remover to remove:
5 Oh, no! it is an ever-fixéd mark,
That looks on tempests and is never shaken;
It is the star to every wandering bark,
Whose worth's unknown, although his height be taken.
Love's not Time's fool, though rosy lips and cheeks
10 Within his bending sickle's compass come;
Love alters not with his brief hours and weeks,
But bears it out even to the edge of doom:
If this be error and upon me proved,
I never writ, nor no man ever loved.

130

My mistress' eyes are nothing like the sun;
Coral is far more red than her lips' red;
If snow be white, why then her breasts are dun;
If hairs be wires, black wires grow on her head.
5 I have seen roses damasked, red and white,
But no such roses see I in her cheeks;
And in some perfumes is there more delight
Than in the breath that from my mistress reeks.
I love to hear her speak, yet well I know
10 That music hath a far more pleasing sound;
I grant I never saw a goddess go;
My mistress, when she walks, treads on the ground.
And yet, by heaven, I think my love as rare
As any she belied with false compare.

William Shakespeare

Since There's No Help

Since there's no help, come let us kiss and part.
    Nay, I have done; you get no more from me,
And I am glad, yea, glad with all my heart,
    That thus so cleanly I myself can free;
5 Shake hands for ever, cancel all our vows,
    And when we meet at any time again,
Be it not seen in either of our brows
    That we one jot of former love retain.
Now at the last gasp of Love's latest breath,
10   When, his pulse failing, Passion speechless lies,
When Faith is kneeling by his bed of death,
    And Innocence is closing up his eyes,
        Now if thou wouldst, when all have given him over,
        From death to life though might'st him yet recover.

Michael Drayton

The Passionate Shepherd to his Love

Come live with me, and be my love,
And we will all the pleasures prove
That valleys, groves, hills and fields,
Woods, or steepy mountain yields.

5 And we will sit upon the rocks,
Seeing the shepherds feed their flocks
By shallow rivers, to whose falls
Melodious birds sing madrigals.

And I will make thee beds of roses,
10 And a thousand fragrant posies,
A cap of flowers, and a kirtle,
Embroidered all with leaves of myrtle.

A gown made of the finest wool
Which from our pretty lambs we pull,
15 Fair linéd slippers for the cold,
With buckles of the purest gold.

A belt of straw and ivy-buds,
With coral clasps and amber studs,
And if these pleasures may thee move,
20 Come live with me, and be my love.

The shepherd swains shall dance and sing
For thy delight each May morning.
If these delights thy mind may move,
Then live with me, and be my love.

Christopher Marlowe

The Nymph's Reply

If all the world and love were young,
And truth in every shepherd's tongue,
These pretty pleasures might me move
To live with thee and be thy love.

5 But Time drives flocks from field to fold,
When rivers rage and rocks grow cold,
And Philomel becometh dumb;
The rest complains of cares to come.

The flowers do fade, and wanton fields
10 To wayward winter reckoning yields;
A honey tongue, a heart of gall
Is fancy's spring, but sorrow's fall.

Thy gowns, thy shoes, thy bed of roses,
Thy cap, thy kirtle, and thy posies,
15 Soon break, soon wither, soon forgotten,
In folly ripe, in reason rotten.

Thy belt of straw and ivy buds,
Thy coral clasps and amber studs,
All these in me no means can move
20 To come to thee and be thy love.

But could youth last and love still breed,
Had joys no date, nor age no need,
Then these delights my mind might move
To live with thee and be thy love.

Sir Walter Raleigh

On Monsieur's Departure

I grieve and dare not show my discontent,
I love and yet am forced to seem to hate,
I do, yet dare not say I ever meant,
I seem stark mute but inwardly do prate.
5   I am and not, I freeze and yet am burned,
       Since from myself another self I turned.

My care is like my shadow in the sun,
Follows me flying, flies when I pursue it,
Stands and lies by me, doth what I have done.
10   His too familiar care doth make me rue it.
       No means I find to rid him from my breast,
       Till by the end of things it be supprest.

Some gentler passion slide into my mind,
For I am soft and made of melting snow;
15   Or be more cruel, love, and so be kind.
Let me or float or sink, be high or low.
       Or let me live with some more sweet content.
       Or die and so forget what love ere meant.

Elizabeth I (attrib.)

Elizabeth I

Mostly Metaphysical Verse

John Donne

To His Coy Mistress

    Had we but world enough, and time,
This coyness, lady, were no crime.
We would sit down, and think which way
To walk, and pass our long love's day.
5 Thou by the Indian Ganges' side
Shoudst rubies find; I by the tide
Of Humber would complain. I would
Love you ten years before the flood,
And you should, if you please, refuse
10 Till the conversion of the Jews.
My vegetable love should grow
Vaster than empires and more slow;
An hundred years should go to praise
Thine eyes, and on thy forehead gaze;
15 Two hundred to adore each breast,
But thirty thousand to the rest;
An age at least to every part,
And the last age should show your heart.
For, lady, you deserve this state,
20 Nor would I love at lower rate.
    But at my back I always hear
Time's wingéd chariot hurrying near;
And yonder all before us lie
Deserts of vast eternity.

25 Thy beauty shall no more be found;
Nor, in thy marble vault, shall sound
My echoing song; then worms shall try
That long-preserved virginity,
And your quaint honour turn to dust,
30 And into ashes all my lust:
The grave's a fine and private place,
But none, I think, do there embrace.
    Now therefore, while the youthful hue
Sits on thy skin like morning glow,
35 And while thy willing soul transpires
At every pore with instant fires,
Now let us sport us while we may,
And now, like amorous birds of prey,
Rather at once our time devour
40 Than languish in his slow-chapped power.
Let us roll all our strength and all
Our sweetness up into one ball,
And tear our pleasures with rough strife
Thorough the iron gates of life:
45 Thus, though we cannot make our sun
Stand still, yet we will make him run.

Andrew Marvell

The Sun Rising

Busy old fool, unruly sun,
        Why dost thou thus
Through windows and through curtains call on us?
Must to thy motions lovers' seasons run?
5   Saucy pedantic wretch, go chide
        Late schoolboys and sour prentices;
    Go tell court-huntsmen that the King will ride;
    Call country ants to harvest offices;
Love, all alike, no season knows nor clime,
10 Nor hours, days, months, which are the rags of time.

        Thy beams so reverend and strong
        Why shouldst thou think?
I could eclipse and cloud them with a wink,
But that I would not lose her sight so long.
15   If her eyes have not blinded thine,
        Look, and tomorrow late, tell me,
    Whether both th' Indias, of spice and mine,
    Be where thou left'st them, or lie here with me.
Ask for those kings whom thou saw'st yesterday,
20 And thou shalt hear, all here in one bed lay.

        She's all states, and all princes I;
        Nothing else is.
Princes do but play us; compared to this,
All honour's mimic, all wealth alchemy.
25   Thou, sun, art half as happy as we,
        In that the world's contracted thus;
    Thine age asks ease, and since thy duties be
    To warm the world, that's done in warming us.
Shine here to us, and thou art everywhere;
30 This bed thy centre is, these walls thy sphere.

John Donne

Death, Be Not Proud

Death, be not proud, though some have callèd thee
Mighty and dreadful, for thou art not so;
For those whom thou think'st thou dost overthrow
Die not, poor Death, nor yet canst thou kill me.
5 From rest and sleep, which but thy pictures be,
Much pleasure; then from thee much more must flow,
And soonest our best men with thee do go,
Rest of their bones, and soul's delivery.
Thou art slave to fate, chance, kings, and desperate men,
10 And dost with poison, war, and sickness dwell,
And poppy, or charms can make us sleep as well
And better than thy stroke; why swell'st thou then?
One short sleep past, we wake eternally
And death shall be no more; Death, thou shalt die.

John Donne

Love

Love bade me welcome: yet my soul drew back,
    Guilty of dust and sin.
But quick-eyed Love, observing me grow slack
    From my first entrance in,
5 Drew nearer to me, sweetly questioning
    If I lacked anything.

"A guest," I answered, "worthy to be here":
    Love said, "You shall be he."
"I, the unkind, ungrateful? Ah, my dear,
10   I cannot look on thee."
Love took my hand, and smiling did reply,
    "Who made the eyes but I?"

"Truth, Lord; but I have marred them; let my shame
    Go where it doth deserve."
15 "And know you not," says Love, "who bore the blame?"
    "My dear, then I will serve."
"You must sit down," says Love, "and taste my meat."
    So I did sit and eat.

George Herbert

To Daffodils

Fair daffodils, we weep to see
    You haste away so soon:
As yet the early-rising sun
    Has not attained his noon.
5   Stay, stay,
    Until the hasting day
       Has run
    But to the evensong;
And, having prayed together, we
10   Will go with you along,

We have short time to stay as you;
    We have as short a spring;
As quick a growth to meet decay,
    As you or anything.
15   We die,
    As your hours do, and dry
       Away
    Like to the summer's rain;
Or as the pearls of morning's dew,
20   Ne'er to be found again.

Robert Herrick

17th Century

Sonnet XVI

When I consider how my light is spent[1]
    Ere half my days, in this dark world and wide,
    And that one talent which is death to hide
    Lodged with me useless, though my soul more bent
5 To serve therewith my Maker, and present
    My true account, lest he returning chide;
    "Doth God exact day-labour, light denied?"
    I fondly[2] ask; but Patience to prevent
That murmur, soon replies, "God doth not need
10 Either man's work or his own gifts; who best
    Bear his mild yoke, they serve him best. His state
Is kingly. Thousands at his bidding speed
    And post o'er land and ocean without rest:
    They also serve who only stand and wait."

John Milton

John Milton

1. Milton had become totally blind in 1651.
2. Foolishly

The World

I saw Eternity the other night
Like a great *Ring* of pure and endless light,
   All calm, as it was bright,
And round beneath it, Time in hours, days, years
5   Driven by the spheres
Like a vast shadow moved, in which the world
   And all her train were hurled;
The doting lover in his quaintest strain
   Did there complain,
10 Near him, his lute, his fancy, and his flights,
   Wit's sour delights,
With gloves, and knots the silly snares of pleasure
   Yet his dear treasure
All scattered lay, while he his eyes did pour
15   Upon a flower.

The darksome states-man hung with weights and woe
Like a thick midnight-fog moved there so slow
   He did nor stay, nor go;
Condemning thoughts (like sad eclipses) scowl
20   Upon his soul,
And clouds of crying witnesses without
   Pyrsued him with one shout.
Yet digged the mole, and lest his ways be found
   Worked under ground,
25 Where he did clutch his prey, but one did see
   That policy,
Churches and altars fed him, perjuries
   Were gnats and flies,
It rained about him blood and tears, but he
30   Drank them as free.

The fearful miser on a heap of rust
Sat pining all his life there, did scarce trust
   His own hands with the dust,
Yet would not place one piece above, but lives
35   In fear of thieves.
Thousands there were as frantic as himself
   And hugged each one his pelf,
The down-right epicure placed heaven in sense
   And scorned pretence
40 While others slipped into a wide excess
   Said little less;
The weaker sort slight, trivial wares enslave
   Who think them brave,
And poor, despised truth sat counting by
45   Their victory.

Yet some, who all this while did weep and sing,
And sing, and weep, soared up into the *Ring*,
   But most would use no wing.
O fools (said I,) thus to prefer dark night
50   Before true light,
To live in grots, and caves, and hate the day
   Because it shows the way,
The way which from this dead and dark abode
   Leads up to God,
55 A way where you might tread the Sun, and be
   More bright than he.
But as I did their madness so discuss
   One whispered thus,
This ring the bride-groom did for none provide
   But for his bride.

I John ii 16–17
All that is in the world, the lust of the flesh, the lust of the eyes, and the pride of life, is not of the father but is of the world.

*   And the world passeth away, and the lusts thereof, but he that doth the will of God abideth for ever.*

Henry Vaughan

The Exequy

Accept, thou shrine of my dead saint,
Instead of dirges, this complaint;
And for sweet flowers to crown thy hearse,
Receive a strew of weeping verse
5 From thy grieved friend, whom thou might'st see
Quite melted into tears for thee.

Dear loss! since thy untimely fate
My task hath been to meditate
On thee, on thee; thou art the book,
10 The library whereon I look,
Though almost blind. For thee, loved clay,
I languish out, not live, the day,
Using no other exercise
But what I practise with mine eyes;
15 By which wet glasses I find out
How lazily time creeps about
To one that mourns: this, only this,
My exercise and business is.
So I compute the weary hours
20 With sighs dissolvéd into showers.

Nor wonder if my time go thus
Backward and most preposterous;
Thou hast benighted me, thy set
This eve of blackness did beget,
25 Who wast my day, though overcast
Before thou hadst thy noontide passed;
And I remember must in tears,
Thou scarce hadst seen so many years
As day tells hours. By thy clear sun
30 My love and fortune first did run;
But thou wilt never more appear
Folded within my hemisphere,
Since both thy light and motïon
Like a fled star is fallen and gone;
35 And 'twixt me and my soul's dear wish
An earth now interposéd is,
Which such a strange eclipse doth make
As ne'er was read in almanac.

I could allow thee for a time
40 To darken me and my sad clime;
Were it a month, a year, or ten,
I would thy exile live till then,
And all that space my mirth adjourn,
So thou wouldst promise to return;
45 And putting off thy ashy shroud,
At length disperse this sorrow's cloud.

But woe is me! the longest date
Too narrow is to calculate
These empty hopes; never shall I
50 Be so much blest as to descry
A glimpse of thee, till that day come
Which shall the earth to cinders doom,
And a fierce fever must calcine
The body of this world – like thine,
55 My little world! That fit of fire
Once off, our bodies shall aspire
To our souls' bliss; then we shall rise
And view ourselves with clearer eyes
In that calm region where no night
60 Can hide us from each other's sight.

Meantime, thou hast her, earth: much good
May my harm do thee. Since it stood
With heaven's will I might not call
Her longer mine, I give thee all
65 My short-lived right and interest
In her whom living I loved best;
With a most free and bounteous grief
I give thee what I could not keep.
Be kind to her, and prithee look
70 Thou write into thy doomsday book
Each parcel of this rarity
Which in thy casket shrined doth lie.
See that thou make thy reckoning straight,
And yield her back again by weight;
75 For thou must audit on thy trust
Each grain and atom of this dust,
As thou wilt answer Him that lent,
Not gave thee, my dear monument.

So close the ground, and 'bout her shade
80 Black curtains draw; my bride is laid.

Sleep on, my love, in thy cold bed,
Never to be disquieted!
My last good-night! Thou wilt not wake
Till I thy fate shall overtake;
85 Till age, or grief, or sickness must
Marry my body to that dust
It so much loves; and fill the room
My heart keeps empty in thy tomb.
Stay for me there; I will not fail
90 To meet thee in that hollow vale.
And think not much of my delay;
I am already on the way,

And follow thee with all the speed
Desire can make, or sorrows breed.
95 Each minute is a short degree,
And every hour a step towards thee.
At night when I betake to rest,
Next morn I rise nearer my west
Of life, almost by eight hours' sail,
100 Than when sleep breathed his drowsy gale.

Thus from the sun my bottom steers,
And my day's compass downward bears;
Nor labour I to stem the tide
Through which to thee I swiftly glide.

105 'Tis true, with shame and grief I yield,
Thou like the van first took'st the field,
And gotten hast the victory

In thus adventuring to die
Before me, whose more years might crave
110 A just precédence in the grave.
But hark! my pulse like a soft drum
Beats my approach, tells thee I come;
And slow howe'er my marches be,
I shall at last sit down by thee.

115 The thought of this bids me go on,
And wait my dissolutiön
With hope and comfort. Dear (forgive
The crime), I am content to live
Divided, with but half a heart,
120 Till we shall meet and never part.

Henry King

To Althea, From Prison

When Love with unconfinéd wings
Hovers within my gates,
And my divine Althea brings
To whisper at the grates;
5 When I lie tangled in her hair
And fettered to her eye,
The gods that wanton in the air
Know no such liberty.

When flowing cups run swiftly round,
10 With no allaying Thames,
Our careless heads with roses bound,
Our hearts with loyal flames;
When thirsty grief in wine we steep,
When healths and draughts go free,
15 Fishes, that tipple in the deep,
Know no such liberty.

When, like committed linnets, I
With shriller throat shall sing
The sweetness, mercy, majesty,
20 And glories of my King;
When I shall voice aloud how good
He is, how great should be,
Enlargéd winds, that curl the flood,
Know no such liberty.

25 Stone walls do not a prison make,
Nor iron bars a cage;
Minds innocent and quiet take
That for an hermitage.
If I have freedom in my love,
30 And in my soul am free,
Angels alone, that soar above,
Enjoy such liberty.

Richard Lovelace

18th Century

Verses on the Death of Dr Swift

Jonathan Swift

    The time is not remote, when I
Must by the course of nature die:
When I foresee my special friends,
Will try to find their private ends:
5 Though it is hardly understood,
Which way my death can do them good;
Yet, thus methinks, I hear 'em speak;
'See, how the Dean begins to break:
Poor gentleman, he droops apace,
10 You plainly find it in his face:
That old vertigo in his head,
Will never leave him, till he's dead:
Besides, his memory decays,
He recollects not what he says;
15 He cannot call his friends to mind;
Forgets the place where last he dined:
Plies you with stories o'er and o'er,
He told them fifty times before.

    How does he fancy we can sit,
20 To hear his out-of-fashioned wit?
But he takes up with younger folks,
Who for his wine will bear his jokes:
Faith, he must make his stories shorter,
Or change his comrades once a quarter:
25 In half the time, he talks them round;
There must another set be found.

    'For poetry, he's past his prime,
He takes an hour to find a rhyme:
His fire is out, his wit decayed,
30 His fancy sunk, his muse a jade.
I'd have him throw away his pen;
But there's no talking to some men.'

    And, then their tenderness appears,
By adding largely to my years:
35 'He's older than he would be reckoned,
And well remembers Charles the Second.

    'He hardly drinks a pint of wine;
And that, I doubt, is no good sign.
His stomach too begins to fail:
40 Last year we thought him strong and hale;
But now, he's quite another thing;
I wish he may hold out till spring.'

    Then hug themselves, and reason thus;
'It is not yet so bad with us.'

45   In such a case they talk in tropes,
And, by their fears express their hopes:
Some great misfortune to portend,
No enemy can match a friend;
With all the kindness they profess,
50 The merit of a lucky guess,
(When daily 'Howd'y's' come of course,
And servants answer: 'Worse and worse')
Would please 'em better than to tell,
That, God be praised, the Dean is well.
55 Then he who prophesied the best,
Approves his foresight to the rest:
'You know, I always feared the worst,
And often told you so at first':
He'd rather choose that I should die,
60 Than his prediction prove a lie.
No one foretells I shall recover;
But, all agree, to give me over.

Yet should some neighbour feel a pain,
Just in the parts, where I complain;
65 How many a message would he send?
What hearty prayers that I should mend?
Enquire what regimen I kept;
What gave me ease, and how I slept?
And more lament, when I was dead,
70 Than all the snivellers round my bed.

My good companions, never fear,
For though you may mistake a year;
Though your prognostics run too fast,
They must be verified at last.

75 'Behold the fatal day arrive!
How is the Dean? He's just alive.
Now the departing prayer is read:
He hardly breathes. The Dean is dead.
Before the passing-bell begun,
80 The news through half the town has run.
O, may we all for death prepare!
What has he left? And who's his heir?
I know no more than what the news is,
'Tis all bequeathed to public uses.
85 To public use! A perfect whim!
What had the public done for him?
Mere envy, avarice, and pride!
He gave it all. – But first he died.
And had the Dean, in all the nation,
90 No worthy friend, no poor relation?
So ready to do strangers good,
Forgetting his own flesh and blood?'

Now Grub Street wits are all employed;
With elegies, the town is cloyed:
95 Some paragraph in every paper,
To curse the Dean, or bless the Drapier.

The doctors tender of their fame,
Wisely on me lay all the blame:
'We must confess his case was nice;
100 But he would never take advice;
Had he been ruled, for aught appears,
He might have lived these twenty years:
For when we opened him we found,
That all his vital parts were sound.'

105 From Dublin soon to London spread,
'Tis told at court, the Dean is dead.

Kind Lady Suffolk in the spleen,
Runs laughing up to tell the Queen.
The Queen, so gracious, mild, and good,
110 Cries, 'Is he gone? 'Tis time he should.
He's dead you say, why let him rot;
I'm glad the medals were forgot.
I promised them, I own; but when?
I only was a princess then;
115 But now as consort of the King,
You know 'tis quite a different thing.'

Here shift the scene, to represent
How those I love, my death lament.
Poor Pope will grieve a month; and Gay
120 A week; and Arbuthnot a day.

St John himself will scarce forbear,
To bite his pen, and drop a tear.
The rest will give a shrug and cry
'I'm sorry; but we all must die.'
125 Indifference clad in wisdom's guise,
All fortitude of mind supplies:
For how can stony bowels melt,
In those who never pity felt;
When *we* are lashed, *they* kiss the rod;
130 Resigning to the will of God.

The fools, my juniors by a year,
Are tortured with suspense and fear.
Who wisely thought my age a screen,
When death approached, to stand between:
135 The screen removed, their hearts are trembling,
They mourn for me without dissembling.

My female friends, whose tender hearts
Have better learnt to act their parts,
Receive the news in doleful dumps,
140 'The Dean is dead, (*and what is trumps?*)
Then Lord have mercy on his soul.
(*Ladies, I'll venture for the vole.*)
Six deans they say must bear the pall.
(*I wish I knew which king to call.*)'
145 'Madam, your husband will attend
The funeral of so good a friend.'
'No madam, 'tis a shocking sight,
And he's engaged tomorrow night!
My Lady Club would take it ill,
150 If he should fail her at quadrille.
He loved the Dean. (*I lead a heart.*)

But dearest friends, they say, must part.
His time was come, he ran his race;
We hope he's in a better place.'

155   Why do we grieve that friends should die?
No loss more easy to supply.
One year is past; a different scene;
No further mention of the Dean;
Who now, alas, no more is missed,
160 Than if he never did exist.
Where's now this favourite of Apollo?
Departed; and his works must follow:
Must undergo the common fate;
His kind of wit is out of date.
165 Some country squire to Lintot goes,
Inquires for Swift in verse and prose:
Says Lintot, 'I have heard the name:
He died a year ago.' The same.
He searcheth all his shop in vain;
170 'Sir, you may find them in Duck Lane:
I sent them with a load of books,
Last Monday to the pastry-cook's.
To fancy they could live a year!
I find you're but a stranger here.
175 The Dean was famous in his time;
And had a kind of knack at rhyme:
His way of writing now is past;
The town hath got a better taste:
I keep no antiquated stuff;
180 But, spick and span I have enough.

'Here's Woolston's tracts, the twelfth edition;
'Tis read by every politician:
The country members, when in town,
To all their boroughs send them down:
185 You never met a thing so smart;
The courtiers have them all by heart:
Those maids of honour (who can read)
Are taught to use them for their creed.
The reverend author's good intention,
190 Hath been rewarded with a pension:
He doth an honour to his gown,
By bravely running priestcraft down:
He shows, as sure as God's in Gloucester,
That Jesus was a grand imposter:
195 That all his miracles were cheats,
Performed as jugglers do their feats:
The church had never such a writer:
A shame he hath not got a mitre!'

200 Suppose me dead; and then suppose
A club assembled at the Rose;
Where from discourse of this and that,
I grow the subject of their chat.
And, while they toss my name about,
With favour some, and some without;
205 One quite indifferent in the cause,
My character impartial draws:

    'The Dean, if we believe report,
Was never ill received at court:
As for his works in verse and prose,
210 I own myself no judge of those:
Nor, can I tell what critics thought 'em;
But, this I know, all people bought 'em;
As with a moral view designed
To cure the vices of mankind:
215 His vein, ironically grave,
Exposed the fool, and lashed the knave:
To steal a hint was never known,
But what he writ was all his own.

    'He never thought an honour done him,
220 Because a duke was proud to own him:
Would rather slip aside, and choose
To talk with wits in dirty shoes:
Despised the fools with stars and garters,
So often seen caressing Chartres.

225   'In exile with a steady heart,
He spent his life's declining part;
Where folly, pride, and faction sway,
Remote from St John, Pope, and Gay.

    'His friendship there to few confined,
230 Were always of the middling kind:
No fools of rank, a mongrel breed,
Who fain would pass for lords indeed:
Where titles give no right or power,
And peerage is a withered flower,
235 He would have held it a disgrace,
If such a wretch had known his face.
On rural squires, that kingdom's bane,
He vented oft his wrath in vain:
Biennial squires, to market brought;
240 Who sell their souls and votes for naught;
The nation stripped, go joyful back,
To rob the church, their tenants rack,
Go snacks with thieves and rapparees,
And keep the peace, to pick up fees:

245 In every job to have a share,
A gaol or barrack to repair;
And turn the tax for public roads
Commodious to their own abodes.

'Perhaps I may allow the Dean
250 Had too much satire in his vein;
And seemed determined not to starve it,
Because no age could more deserve it.
Yet, malice never was his aim;
He lashed the vice but spared the name.
255 No individual could resent,
Where thousands equally were meant.
His satire points at no defect,
But what all mortals may correct;
For he abhorred that senseless tribe,
260 Who call it humour when they jibe:
He spared a hump or crooked nose,
Whose owners set not up for beaux.
True genuine dullness moved his pity,

Unless it offered to be witty.
265 Those, who their ignorance confessed,
He ne'er offended with a jest;
But laughed to hear an idiot quote,
A verse from Horace, learnt by rote.

'He knew an hundred pleasant stories,
270 With all the turns of Whigs and Tories:
Was cheerful to his dying day,
And friends would let him have his way.

'He gave the little wealth he had,
To build a house for fools and mad:
275 And showed by one satiric touch,
No nation wanted it so much:
That kingdom he hath left his debtor,
I wish it soon may have a better.'

Jonathan Swift

Elegy Written in a Country Churchyard

The curfew tolls the knell of parting day,
   The lowing herd wind slowly o'er the lea,
The plowman homeward plods his weary way,
   And leaves the world to darkness and to me.

5 Now fades the glimmering landscape on the sight,
   And all the air a solemn stillness holds,
Save where the beetle wheels his droning flight,
   And drowsy tinklings lull the distant folds;

Save that from yonder ivy-mantled tower
10   The moping owl does to the moon complain
Of such, as wandering near her secret bower,
   Molest her ancient solitary reign.

Beneath those rugged elms, that yew tree's shade,
   Where heaves the turf in many a mouldering heap,
15 Each in his narrow cell forever laid,
   The rude forefathers of the hamlet sleep.

The breezy call of incense-breathing morn,
   The swallow twittering from the straw-built shed,
The cock's shrill clarion, or the echoing horn,
20   No more shall rouse them from their lowly bed.

For them no more the blazing hearth shall burn,
   Or busy housewife ply her evening care;
No children run to lisp their sire's return,
   Or climb his knees the envied kiss to share.

25 Oft did the harvest to their sickle yield,
   Their furrow oft the stubborn glebe has broke;
How jocund did they drive their team afield!
   How bowed the woods beneath their sturdy stroke!

Let not Ambition mock their useful toil,
30   Their homely joys, and destiny obscure;
Nor Grandeur hear with a disdainful smile
   The short and simple annals of the poor.

The boast of heraldry, the pomp of power,
   And all that beauty, all that wealth e'er gave,
35 Awaits alike the inevitable hour.
   The paths of glory lead but to the grave.

Nor you, ye proud, impute to these the fault,
   If Memory o'er their tomb no trophies raise,
Where through the long-drawn aisle and fretted vault
40   The pealing anthem swells the note of praise.

Can storied urn or animated bust
   Back to its mansion call the fleeting breath?
Can Honour's voice provoke the silent dust,
   Or Flattery soothe the dull cold ear of Death?

45 Perhaps in this neglected spot is laid
   Some heart once pregnant with celestial fire;
Hands that the rod of empire might have swayed,
   Or waked to ecstasy the living lyre.

But Knowledge to their eyes her ample page
50   Rich with the spoils of time did ne'er unroll;
Chill Penury repressed their noble rage,
   And froze the genial current of the soul.

Full many a gem of purest ray serene,
   The dark unfathomed caves of ocean bear:
55 Full many a flower is born to blush unseen,
   And waste its sweetness on the desert air.

Some village Hampden, that with dauntless breast
   The little tyrant of his fields withstood;
Some mute inglorious Milton here may rest,
60   Some Cromwell guiltless of his country's blood.

The applause of listening senates to command,
   The threats of pain and ruin to despise,
To scatter plenty o'er a smiling land,
   And read their history in a nation's eyes,

65 Their lot forbade: nor circumscribed alone
   Their growing virtues, but their crimes confined;
Forbade to wade through slaughter to a throne,
   And shut the gates of mercy on mankind,

The struggling pangs of conscious truth to hide,
   To quench the blushes of ingenuous shame,
70 Or heap the shrine of Luxury and Pride
   With incense kindled at the Muse's flame.

Far from the madding crowd's ignoble strife,
    Their sober wishes never learned to stray;
75 Along the cool sequestered vale of life
    They kept the noiseless tenor of their way.

Yet even these bones from insult to protect
    Some frail memorial still erected nigh,
With uncouth rhymes and shapeless sculpture decked
80   Implores the passing tribute of a sigh.

Their name, their years, spelt by the unlettered Muse,
    The place of fame and elegy supply:
And many a holy text around she strews,
    That teach the rustic moralist to die.

85 For who to dumb Forgetfulness a prey,
    This pleasing anxious being e'er resigned,
Left the warm precincts of the cheerful day,
    Nor cast one longing lingering look behind?

On some fond breast the parting soul relies,
90   Some pious drops the closing eye requires;
Even from the tomb the voice of Nature cries,
    Even in our ashes live their wonted fires.

For thee, who mindful of the unhonoured dead
    Dost in these lines their artless tale relate;
95 If chance, by lonely contemplation led,
    Some kindred spirit shall inquire thy fate,

Haply some hoary-headed swain may say,
    "Oft have we seen him at the peep of dawn
Brushing with hasty steps the dews away
100   To meet the sun upon the upland lawn.

"There at the foot of yonder nodding beech
    That wreathes its old fantastic roots so high,
His listless length at noontide would he stretch,
    And pore upon the brook that babbles by.

105 "Hard by yon wood, now smiling as in scorn,
    Muttering his wayward fancies he would rove,
Now drooping, woeful wan, like one forlorn,
    Or crazed with care, or crossed in hopeless love.

"One morn I missed him on the customed hill,
110   Along the heath and near his favourite tree;
Another came; nor yet beside the rill,
    Nor up the lawn, nor at the wood was he;

"The next with dirges due in sad array
    Slow through the churchway path we saw him borne.
115 Approach and read (for thou canst read) the lay,
    Graved on the stone beneath yon aged thorn."

The Epitaph
Here rests his head upon the lap of Earth
    A youth to Fortune and to Fame unknown.
Fair Science frowned not on his humble birth,
120   *And Melancholy marked him for her own.*

Large was his bounty, and his soul sincere,
    Heaven did a recompense as largely send:
He gave to Misery all he had, a tear,
    He gained from Heaven ('twas all he wished) a friend.

125 *No farther seek his merits to disclose,*
    Or draw his frailties from their dread abode
(There they alike in trembling hope repose),
    The bosom of his Father and his God.

Thomas Gray

Epistle to Dr Arbuthnot

P. Shut, shut the door, good John! (fatigued, I said),
Tie up the knocker, say I'm sick, I'm dead.
The Dog Star rages! nay 'tis past a doubt
All Bedlam, or Parnassus, is let out:
5   Fire in each eye, and papers in each hand,
They rave, recite, and madden round the land.
    What walls can guard me, or what shades can hide?
They pierce my thickets, through my grot they glide,
By land, by water, they renew the charge,
10 They stop the chariot, and they board the barge.
No place is sacred, not the church is free;
Even Sunday shines no Sabbath day to me:
Then from the Mint walks forth the man of rhyme,
Happy to catch me just at dinner time.
15   Is there a parson, much bemused in beer,
A maudlin poetess, a rhyming peer,
A clerk foredoomed his father's soul to cross,
Who pens a stanza when he should engross?
Is there who, locked from ink and paper, scrawls
20 With desperate charcoal round his darkened walls?
All fly to Twit'nam, and in humble strain
Apply to me to keep them mad or vain.
Arthur, whose giddy son neglects the laws,
Imputes to me and my damned works the cause:
25 Poor Cornus sees his frantic wife elope,
And curses wit, and poetry, and Pope.
    Friend to my life (which did not you prolong,
The world had wanted many an idle song)
What drop or nostrum can this plague remove?
30 Or which must end me, a fool's wrath or love?
A dire dilemma! either way I'm sped,
If foes, they write, if friends, they read me dead.
Seized and tied down to judge, how wretched I!
Who can't be silent, and who will not lie.
35 To laugh were want of goodness and of grace,
And to be grave exceeds all power of face.
I sit with sad civility, I read
With honest anguish and an aching head,
And drop at last, but in unwilling ears,
40 This saving counsel, "Keep your piece nine years."
    "Nine years!" cries he, who high in Drury Lane,
Lulled by soft zephyrs through the broken pane,
Rhymes ere he wakes, and prints before term ends,
Obliged by hunger and request of friends:
45 "The piece, you think, is incorrect? why, take it,
I'm all submission, what you'd have it, make it."
    Three things another's modest wishes bound,
My friendship, and a prologue, and ten pound.

Pitholeon sends to me: "You know his Grace,
50 I want a patron; ask him for a place."
Pitholeon libeled me –"but here's a letter
Informs you, sir, 'twas when he knew no better.
Dare you refuse him? Curll invites to dine,
He'll write a *Journal*, or he'll turn divine.
55 Bless me! a packet. –" 'Tis a stranger sues,
A virgin tragedy, an orphan Muse."
If I dislike it, "Furies, death, and rage!"
If I approve, "Commend it to the stage."
There (thank my stars) my whole commission ends,
60 The players and I are, luckily, no friends.
Fired that the house reject him, " 'Sdeath, I'll print it,
And shame the fools – Your interest, sir, with Lintot!"
Lintot, dull rogue, will think your price too much.
"Not, sir, if you revise it, and retouch."
65 All my demurs but double his attacks;
At last he whispers, "Do; and we go snacks."
Glad of a quarrel, straight I clap the door,
"Sir, let me see your works and you no more."
    'Tis sung, when Midas' ears began to spring
70 (Midas, a sacred person and a king),
His very minister who spied them first
(Some say his queen) was forced to speak, or burst.
And is not mine, my friend, a sorer case,
When every coxcomb perks them in my face?
75   A. Good friend, forbear! you deal in dangerous things.
I'd never name queens, ministers, or kings;
Keep close to ears, and those let asses prick;
'Tis nothing——P. Nothing? if they bite and kick?
Out with it, *Dunciad!* let the secret pass,
80 That secret to each fool, that he's an ass:
The truth once told (and wherefore should we lie?)
The queen of Midas slept, and so may I.
    You think this cruel? take it for a rule,
No creature smarts so little as a fool.
85 Let peals of laughter, Codrus! round thee break,
Thou unconcerned canst hear the mighty crack.
Pit, box, and gallery in convulsions hurled,
Thou stand'st unshook amidst a bursting world.
Who shames a scribbler? break one cobweb through,
90 He spins the slight, self-pleasing thread anew:
Destroy his fib or sophistry, in vain;
The creature's at his dirty work again,
Throned in the centre of his thin designs,
Proud of a vast extent of flimsy lines.
95 Whom have I hurt? has poet yet or peer
Lost the arched eyebrow or Parnassian sneer?
And has not Colley still his lord and whore?
His butchers Henley? his freemasons Moore?

Does not one table Bavius still admit?
100 Still to one bishop Philips seem a wit?
    Still Sappho——A. Hold! for God's sake – you'll offend.
    No names – be calm – learn prudence of a friend.
    I too could write, and I am twice as tall;
    But foes like these!——P. One flatterer's worse than all.
105 Of all mad creatures, if the learn'd are right,
    It is the slaver kills, and not the bite.
    A fool quite angry is quite innocent:
    Alas! 'tis ten times worse when they repent.
        One dedicates in high heroic prose,
110 And ridicules beyond a hundred foes;
    One from all Grub Street will my fame defend,
    And, more abusive, calls himself my friend.
    This prints my letters, that expects a bribe,
    And others roar aloud, "Subscribe, subscribe!"
115   There are, who to my person pay their court:
    I cough like Horace, and, though lean, am short;
    Ammon's great son one shoulder had too high,
    Such Ovid's nose, and "Sir! you have an eye –"
    Go on, obliging creatures, make me see
120 All that disgraced my betters met in me.
    Say for my comfort, languishing in bed,
    "Just so immortal Maro held his head":
    And when I die, be sure you let me know
    Great Homer died three thousand years ago.
125   Why did I write? what sin to me unknown
    Dipped me in ink, my parents', or my own?
    As yet a child, nor yet a fool to fame,
    I lisped in numbers, for the numbers came.
    I left no calling for this idle trade,
130 No duty broke, no father disobeyed.
    The Muse but served to ease some friend, not wife,
    To help me through this long disease, my life,
    To second, Arbuthnot! thy art and care,
    And teach the being you preserved, to bear.
135   A. But why then publish? P. Granville the polite,
    And knowing Walsh, would tell me I could write;
    Well-natured Garth inflamed with early praise,
    And Congreve loved, and Swift endured my lays;
    The courtly Talbot, Somers, Sheffield, read;
140 Even mitred Rochester would nod the head,
    And St. John's self (great Dryden's friends before)
    With open arms received one poet more.
    Happy my studies, when by these approved!
    Happier their author, when by these beloved!
145 From these the world will judge of men and books,
    Not from the Burnets, Oldmixons, and Cookes.
        Soft were my numbers; who could take offence
    While pure description held the place of sense?

Like gentle Fanny's was my flowery theme,
150 A painted mistress, or a purling stream.
Yet then did Gildon draw his venal quill;
I wished the man a dinner, and sat still.
Yet then did Dennis rave in furious fret;
I never answered, I was not in debt.
155 If want provoked, or madness made them print,
I waged no war with Bedlam or the Mint.
    Did some more sober critic come abroad?
If wrong, I smiled; if right, I kissed the rod.
Pains, reading, study are their just pretence,
160 And all they want is spirit, taste, and sense.
Commas and points they set exactly right,
And 'twere a sin to rob them of their mite.
Yet ne'er one sprig of laurel graced these ribalds,
From slashing Bentley down to piddling Tibbalds.
165 Each wight who reads not, and but scans and spells,
Each word-catcher that lives on syllables,
Even such small critics some regard may claim,
Preserved in Milton's or in Shakespeare's name.
Pretty! in amber to observe the forms
170 Of hairs, or straws, or dirt, or grubs, or worms!
The things, we know, are neither rich nor rare,
But wonder how the devil they got there.
    Were others angry? I excused them too;
Well might they rage; I gave them but their due.
175 A man's true merit 'tis not hard to find;
But each man's secret standard in his mind,
That casting weight pride adds to emptiness,
This, who can gratify? for who can guess?
The bard whom pilfered pastorals renown,
180 Who turns a Persian tale for half a crown,
Just writes to make his barrenness appear,
And strains from hard-bound brains eight lines a year:
He, who still wanting, though he lives on theft,
Steals much, spends little, yet has nothing left;
185 And he who now to sense, now nonsense leaning,
Means not, but blunders round about a meaning:
And he whose fustian's so sublimely bad,
It is not poetry, but prose run mad:
All these, my modest satire bade translate,
190 And owned that nine such poets made a Tate.
How did they fume, and stamp, and roar, and chafe!
And swear, not Addison himself was safe.
    Peace to all such! but were there one whose fires
True Genius kindles, and fair Fame inspires;
195 Blessed with each talent and each art to please,
And born to write, converse, and live with ease:
Should such a man, too fond to rule alone,
Bear, like the Turk, no brother near the throne;

View him with scornful, yet with jealous eyes,
200　And hate for arts that caused himself to rise;
　　　Damn with faint praise, assent with civil leer,
　　　And without sneering, teach the rest to sneer;
　　　Willing to wound, and yet afraid to strike,
　　　Just a hint a fault, and hesitate dislike;
205　Alike reserved to blame or to commend,
　　　A timorous foe, and a suspicious friend;
　　　Dreading even fools; by flatterers besieged,
　　　And so obliging that he ne'er obliged;
　　　Like Cato, give his little senate laws,
210　And sit attentive to his own applause;
　　　While wits and Templars every sentence raise,
　　　And wonder with a foolish face of praise –
　　　Who but must laugh, if such a man there be?
　　　Who would not weep, if Atticus were he?
215　　　What though my name stood rubric on the walls?
　　　Or plastered posts, with claps, in capitals?
　　　Or smoking forth, a hundred hawkers' load,
　　　On wings of winds came flying all abroad?
　　　I sought no homage from the race that write;
220　I kept, like Asian monarchs, from their sight;
　　　Poems I heeded (now berhymed so long)
　　　No more than thou, great George! a birthday song.
　　　I ne'er with wits or witlings passed my days
　　　To spread about the itch of verse and praise;
225　Nor like a puppy daggled through the town
　　　To fetch and carry sing-song up and down;
　　　Nor at rehearsals sweat, and mouthed, and cried,
　　　With handkerchief and orange at my side;
　　　But sick of fops, and poetry, and prate,
230　To Bufo left the whole Castalian state.
　　　　　Proud as Apollo on his forkéd hill,
　　　Sat full-blown Bufo, puffed by every quill;
　　　Fed with soft dedication all day long,
　　　Horace and he went hand in hand in song.
235　His library (where busts of poets dead
　　　And a true Pindar stood without a head)
　　　Received of wits an undistinguished race,
　　　Who first his judgment asked, and then a place:
　　　Much they extolled his pictures, much his seat,
240　And flattered every day, and some days eat:
　　　Till grown more frugal in his riper days,
　　　He paid some bards with port, and some with praise;
　　　To some a dry rehearsal was assigned,
　　　And others (harder still) he paid in kind.
245　Dryden alone (what wonder?) came not nigh;
　　　Dryden alone escaped this judging eye:
　　　But still the great have kindness in reserve;
　　　He helped to bury whom he helped to starve.

May some choice patron bless each gray goose quill!
250 May every Bavius have his Bufo still!
Or when a statesman wants a day's defence,
Or Envy holds a whole week's war with Sense,
Or simple Pride for flattery makes demands,
May dunce by dunce be whistled off my hands!
255 Blessed be the great! for those they take away,
And those they left me – for they left me Gay;
Left me to see neglected genius bloom,
Neglected die, and tell it on his tomb;
Of all thy blameless life the sole return
260 My verse, and Queensberry weeping o'er thy urn!
Oh, let me live my own, and die so too!
("To live and die is all I have to do")
Maintain a poet's dignity and ease,
And see what friends, and read what books I please;
265 Above a patron, though I condescend
Some times to call a minister my friend.
I was not born for courts or great affairs;
I pay my debts, believe, and say my prayers,
Can sleep without a poem in my head,
270 Nor know if Dennis be alive or dead.
    Why am I asked what next shall see the light?
Heavens! was I born for nothing but to write?
Has life no joys for me? or (to be grave)
Have I no friend to serve, no soul to save?
275 "I found him close with Swift"–"Indeed? no doubt,"
Cries prating Balbus, "something will come out."
'Tis all in vain, deny it as I will.
"No, such a genius never can lie still,"
And then for mine obligingly mistakes
280 The first lampoon Sir Will or Bubo makes.
Poor guiltless I! and can I choose but smile,
When every coxcomb knows me by my style?
    Cursed be the verse, how well soe'er it flow,
That tends to make one worthy man my foe,
285 Give Virtue scandal, Innocence a fear,
Or from the soft-eyed virgin steal a tear!
But he who hurts a harmless neighbour's peace,
Insults fallen worth, or Beauty in distress,
Who loves a lie, lame Slander helps about,
290 Who writes a libel, or who copies out:
That fop whose pride affects a patron's name,
Yet absent, wounds an author's honest fame;
Who can your merit selfishly approve,
And show the sense of it without the love;
295 Who has the vanity to call you friend,
Yet wants the honour, injured, to defend;
Who tells whate'er you think, whate'er you say,
And, if he lie not, must at least betray:

74

Who to the dean and silver bell can swear,
300 And sees at Cannons what was never there:
Who reads but with a lust to misapply,
Make satire a lampoon, and fiction, lie:
A lash like mine no honest man shall dread,
But all such babbling blockheads in his stead.
305   Let Sporus tremble—— A. What? that thing of silk,
Sporus, that mere white curd of ass's milk?
Satire or sense, alas! can Sporus feel?
Who breaks a butterfly upon a wheel?
        P. Yet let me flap this bug with gilded wings,
310 This painted child of dirt, that stinks and stings;
Whose buzz the witty and fair annoys,
Yet wit ne'er tastes, and beauty ne'er enjoys;
So well-bred spaniels civilly delight
In mumbling of the game they dare not bite.
315 Eternal smiles his emptiness betray,
As shallow streams run dimpling all the way.
Whether in florid impotence he speaks,
And, as the prompter breathes, the puppet squeaks;
Or at the ear of Eve, familiar toad,
320 Half froth, half venom, spits himself abroad,
In puns, or politics, or tales, or lies,
Or spite, or smut, or rhymes, or blasphemies.
His wit all seesaw between *that* and *this*,
Now high, now low, now master up, now miss,
325 And he himself one vile antithesis.
Amphibious thing! that acting either part,
The trifling head or the corrupted heart,
Fop at the toilet, flatterer at the board,
Now trips a lady, and now struts a lord.
330 Eve's tempter thus the rabbins have expressed,
A cherub's face, a reptile all the rest;
Beauty that shocks you, parts that none will trust,
Wit that can creep, and pride that licks the dust.
        Not Fortune's worshiper, nor Fashion's fool,
335 Not Lucre's madman, nor Ambition's tool,
Not proud, nor servile, be one poet's praise,
That if he pleased, he pleased by manly ways:
That flattery, even to kings, he held a shame,
And thought a lie in verse or prose the same:
340 That not in fancy's maze he wandered long,
But stooped to truth, and moralized his song:
That not for fame, but Virtue's better end,
He stood the furious foe, the timid friend,
The damning critic, half approving wit,
345 The coxcomb hit, or fearing to be hit;
Laughed at the loss of friends he never had,
The dull, the proud, the wicked, and the mad;
The distant threats of vengeance on his head,

The blow unfelt, the tear he never shed;
350　The tale revived, the lie so oft o'erthrown,
The imputed trash, and dullness not his own;
The morals blackened when the writings 'scape,
The libeled person, and the pictured shape;
Abuse on all he loved, or loved him, spread,
355　A friend in exile, or a father dead;
The whisper, that to greatness still too near,
Perhaps yet vibrates on his sovereign's ear –
Welcome for thee, fair Virtue! all the past!
For thee, fair Virtue! welcome even the last!

360　　A. But why insult the poor, affront the great?
P. A knave's a knave to me in every state:
Alike my scorn, if he succeed or fail,
Sporus at court, or Japhet in a jail,
A hireling scribbler, or a hireling peer,
365　Knight of the post corrupt, or of the shire,
If on a pillory, or near a throne,
He gain his prince's ear, or lose his own.
　　Yet soft by nature, more a dupe than wit,
Sappho can tell you how this man was bit:
370　This dreaded satirist Dennis will confess
Foe to his pride, but friend to his distress:
So humble, he has knocked at Tibbald's door,
Has drunk with Cibber, nay, has rhymed for Moore.
Full ten years slandered, did he once reply?
375　Three thousand suns went down on Welsted's lie.
To please a mistress one aspersed his life;
He lashed him not, but let her be his wife.
Let Budgell charge low Grub Street on his quill,
And write whate'er he pleased, except his will;
380　Let the two Curlls, of town and court, abuse
His father, mother, body, soul, and muse.
Yet why? that father held it for a rule,
It was a sin to call our neighbor fool;
That harmless mother thought no wife a whore:
385　Hear this, and spare his family, James Moore!
Unspotted names, and memorable long,
If there be force in virtue, or in song.
　　Of gentle blood (part shed in honour's cause,
While yet in Britain honour had applause)
390　Each parent sprung—— A. What fortune, pray?—— P. Their own,
And better got than Bestia's from the throne.
Born to no pride, inheriting no strife,
Nor marrying discord in a noble wife,
Stranger to civil and religious rage,
395　The good man walked innoxious through his age.
No courts he saw, no suits would every try,
Nor dared an oath, nor hazarded a lie.

Unlearn'd, he knew no schoolman's subtle art,
No language but the language of the heart.
405 By nature honest, by experience wise,
Healthy by temperance, and by exercise;
His life, though long, to sickness passed unknown,
His death was instant, and without a groan.
Oh, grant me thus to live, and thus to die!
410 Who sprung from kings shall know less joy than I.
        O friend! may each domestic bliss be thine!
Be no unpleasing melancholy mine:
Me, let the tender office long engage,
To rock the cradle of reposing Age,
415 With lenient arts extend a mother's breath,
Make Languor smile, and smooth the bed of Death,
Explore the thought, explain the asking eye,
And keep a while one parent from the sky!
On cares like these if length of days attend,
420 May Heaven, to bless those days, preserve my friend,
Preserve him social, cheerful, and serene,
And just as rich as when he served a Queen!
A. Whether that blessing be denied or given,
Thus far was right – the rest belongs to Heaven.

Alexander Pope

The Emulation

Say, tyrant Custom, why must we obey
The impositions of thy haughty sway?
From the first dawn of life unto the grave,
Poor womankind's in every state a slave,
5   The nurse, the mistress, parent and the swain,
For love she must, there's none escape that pain.
Then comes the last, the fatal slavery:
The husband with insulting tyranny
Can have ill manners justified by law,
10 For men all join to keep the wife in awe.
Moses, who first our freedom did rebuke,
Was married when he writ the Pentateuch.
They're wise to keep us slaves, for well they know,
If we were loose, we soon should make them so.
15 We yield like vanquished kings whom fetters bind,
When chance of war is to usurpers kind;
Submit in form; but they'd our thoughts control,
And lay restraints on the impassive soul.
They fear we should excel their sluggish parts,
20 Should we attempt the sciences and arts;
Pretend they were designed for them alone,
So keep us fools to raise their own renown.
Thus priests of old, their grandeur to maintain,
Cried vulgar eyes would sacred laws profane;
25 So kept the mysteries behind a screen:
Their homage and the name were lost had they been seen.
But in this blessèd age such freedom's given,
That every man explains the will of heaven;
And shall we women now sit tamely by,
30 Make no excursions in philosophy,
Or grace our thoughts in tuneful poetry?
We will our rights in learning's world maintain;
Wit's empire now shall know a female reign.
Come, all ye fair, the great attempt improve,
35 Divinely imitate the realms above:
There's ten celestial females govern wit,
And but two gods that dare pretend to it.
And shall these finite males reverse their rules?
No, we'll be wits, and then men must be fools.

Sarah Egerton

Ode to Evening

If aught of oaten stop, or pastoral song,
May hope, chaste Eve, to soothe thy modest ear,
   Like thy own solemn springs,
   Thy springs and dying gales,
5 O nymph reserved, while now the bright-haired sun
Sits in yon western tent, whose cloudy skirts,
   With brede ethereal wove,
   O'erhang his wavy bed:
Now air is hushed, save where the weak-eyed bat,
10 With short shrill shriek flits by on leathern wing,
   Or where the beetle winds
   His small but sullen horn,
As oft he rises 'midst the twilight path,
Against the pilgrim borne in heedless hum:
15   Now teach me, maid composed,
   To breathe some softened strain,
Whose numbers, stealing through thy darkening vale,
May not unseemly with its stillness suit,
   As, musing slow, I hail
20   Thy genial loved return!
For when the folding-star arising shows
His paly circlet, at his warning lamp
   The fragrant Hours, and elves
   Who slept in flowers the day,
25 And many a nymph who wreaths her brows with sedge,
And sheds the freshening dew, and, lovelier still,
   The pensive Pleasures sweet,

   Prepare thy shadowy car.
Then lead, calm votaress, where some sheety lake
30 Cheers the lone heath, or some time-hallowed pile
   Or upland fallows gray
   Reflect its last cool gleam.
But when chill blustering winds, or driving rain,
Forbid my willing feet, be mine the hut
35   That from the mountain's side
   Views wilds, and swelling floods,
And hamlets brown, and dim-discovered spires,
And hears their simple bell, and marks o'er all
   Thy dewy fingers draw
40   The gradual dusky veil.
While Spring shall pour his showers, as oft he wont,
And bathe thy breathing tresses, meekest Eve;
   While Summer loves to sport
   Beneath thy lingering light;
45 While sallow Autumn fills thy lap with leaves;
Or Winter, yelling through the troublous air,
   Affrights thy shrinking train,
   And rudely rends thy robes;
So long, sure-found beneath the sylvan shed,
50 Shall Fancy, Friendship, Science, rose-lipped Health,
   Thy gentlest influence own,
   And hymn thy favourite name!

William Collins

Acknowledgements

W H Auden: 'O What is That Sound' from *Collected Poems*, reprinted by permission of the publishers, Faber & Faber Ltd.

Margaret Atwood: 'This is a Photograph of Me' from *Poems 1965–1975* (Virago Press, 1975), reprinted by permission of Little Brown.

James K Baxter: 'New Zealand' from *Collected Poems of James K Baxter* (OUP Australia and New Zealand)

Patricia Beer: 'Abbey Tomb' from *Collected Poems* (Carcanet, 1990), reprinted by permission of Carcanet Press Ltd.

Sujata Bhatt: 'Maninagar Days' from *Monkey Shadows* (Carcanet, 1991), reprinted by permission of Carcanet Press Ltd.

Gillian Clarke: 'Marged' from *Collected Poems* (Carcanet, 1997), reprinted by permission of Carcanet Press Ltd.

Merle Collins: 'Callaloo' reprinted by permission of Curtis Brown Ltd, London, on behalf of the author.

Helen Dunmore: 'All the Things You Are Not Yet' from *Bestiary* (Bloodaxe Books, 1997), reprinted by permission of the publisher.

T S Eliot: 'The Love Song of J Alfred Prufrock' from *Collected Poems 1909–1962*, reprinted by permission of the publishers, Faber & Faber Ltd.

Eleanor Farjeon: 'Easter Monday' from *First and Second Love* (Michael Joseph, 1949) reprinted by permission of David Higham Associates.

Ted Hughes: 'Wuthering Heights' from *The Birthday Letters* (1998), reprinted by permission of the publishers, Faber & Faber Ltd.

Rudyard Kipling: 'The Way Through the Woods' from *Rudyard Kipling's Verse: The Definitive Edition* (Hodder & Stoughton, 1945), by permission of A P Watt Ltd on behalf of The National Trust for Places of Historic Interest or Natural Beauty.

Philip Larkin: 'An Arundel Tomb' from *Collected Poems*, reprinted by permission of the publishers, Faber & Faber Ltd.

Louis MacNeice: 'Prayer Before Birth' from *Collected Poems* (Faber), reprinted by permission of David Higham Associates.

Grace Nichols: 'Iguana Memory' from *The Fat Black Woman's Poems* (Virago Press, 1984), copyright © Grace Nichols 1984, reprinted by permission of Curtis Brown Ltd, London on behalf of the author.

Sylvia Plath: 'Wuthering Heights' from *Collected Poems*, reprinted by permission of the publishers, Faber & Faber Ltd.

Al Purdy: 'Trees at the Arctic Circle' from *Being Alive* (McClelland & Stewart, 1980), reprinted by permission of the author.

Dylan Thomas: 'Do Not Go Gentle into that Good Night' from *Collected Poems* (J M Dent), reprinted by permission of David Higham Associates.

R S Thomas: 'Here' from *Collected Poems* (J M Dent), reprinted by permission of the Orion Publishing Group.

Derek Walcott: 'Oddjob, a Bull Terrier' from *Sea Grapes* (Jonathan Cape, 1976), reprinted by permission of The Random House Group Ltd.

W B Yeats: 'The Second Coming' from *Collected Poems* (Macmillan), by permission of A P Watt on behalf of Michael B Yeats.

Despite every effort to trace and contact copyright holders prior to publication this has not been possible in all cases. The publishers undertake to rectify any errors or omissions at the earliest opportunity.

Photo acknowledgements
Gillian Clarke by Susan Butler.
Grace Nichols by Fanny Dubes.
All other portraits from Mary Evans Picture Library.

ISBN 10: 0 19 831472 8
ISBN 13: 978 0 19 831472 1

© London Qualifications Ltd. 2003
Reprinted 2000, 2001, 2002, 2003, 2005, 2006
Published by Edexcel
        Stewart House
        32 Russell Square
        London WC1B 5DN
Produced by Oxford University Press
Typeset and designed by Zed, Oxford
Printed by WM Print Ltd., Walsall